# PARIS BY RAIL TRAVEL GUIDE 2024-2025

By

Graham Vishai

Copyright © (Graham Vishai) 2024. All rights reserved

Before this document is duplicated or reproduced in any manner, the publisher's consent must be gained.

Therefore, the contents within can neither be stored electronically, transferred, nor kept in a database. Neither in part nor in full can the document be copied, scanned, faxed, or retained without approval from the publisher or creator.

Hello for the purpose of this travel guide no images or maps are included, but only to bring it to your attention and also to give you the best description and information.

I hope you guys find whatever you are looking for in your own personal view.

# Table of Contents

**Acknowledgment:**
**Dedication:**
**Chapter 1 Introduction**
    1.1 Welcome to Paris by Rail
    1.2 Why Choose Rail Travel for Exploring Paris
    1.3 How to Use This Guide
**Chapter 2 Getting Ready**
    2.1 Planning Your Trip to Paris by Rail
    2.2 Choosing the Right Time to Visit
    2.3 Booking Rail Tickets and Passes
    2.4 Currency and money matters
    2.5 Packing Tips for Rail Travel
**Chapter 3 Arriving in Paris**
    3.1 Arriving at Gare du Nord: Your Gateway to Paris
    3.2 How to arrive in Paris via train from any part of the world
    3.3 Navigating the Train Station
    3.4 Connecting to the Metro and Other Public Transport

**Chapter 4 Exploring Paris by Rail**
    4.1 Understanding Parisian Rail Network
    4.2 Overview of RER, Metro, and Tram Systems
    4.3 Types of Tickets and Passes
    4.4 Tips for Navigating Parisian Rail System

**Chapter 5 Must-Visit Landmarks and Attractions**
    5.1 Eiffel Tower
    5.2 Louvre Museum
    5.3 Notre-Dame Cathedral
    5.4 Champs-Élysées
    5.5 Montmartre
    5.6 Seine River Cruise
    5.7  More Hidden Gems

**Chapter 6 Day Trips from Paris**
    6.1 Versailles: The Palace and Gardens
    6.2 Getting to Versailles by Train
    6.3 Exploring the Palace and Grounds
    6.4 Disneyland Paris: A Magical Day Out
    6.5 Trains to Disneyland
    6.6 Tips for Enjoying Disneyland Paris by Rail
    6.7 Giverny: Monet's Garden
    6.8 Visiting Giverny by Rail
    6.9 Exploring Monet's Home and Gardens

**Chapter 7 Experiencing Parisian Culture**
    7.1 Parisian Cuisine: Foodie's Guide by Rail
    7.2 French Culinary Delights to Try
    7.3 Best Restaurants and Cafés Accessible by Rail
    7.4 Shopping in Paris: Chic Boutiques and Markets
    7.5 Retail Therapy by Rail

7.6 Unique Souvenirs to Bring Home

**Chapter 8 Staying in Paris**

8.1 Finding the Perfect Accommodation by Rail

8.2 Hotels and guests houses near train station in Paris and their prices per night

8.3 Airbnb and Other Accommodation Options

**Chapter 9 Safety and Practical Tips**

9.1 Staying Safe in Paris

9.2 Insights on Common Scams

9.3 Emergency Contacts

9.4 Useful French Phrases for Rail Travelers

9.5 Basic Phrases for Navigating Paris

9.6 Glossary of train and rail terms

**Chapter 10 Appendices**

10.1 Sample Rail Itineraries for Different Lengths of Stay

10.2 Rail Maps and Timetables

10.3 Glossary of Parisian Rail Travel Terms

**Chapter 11 Conclusion**

11.1 Make the Most of Your Paris Adventure by Rail

11.2 Reminiscing Your Time in Paris

11.3 Feedback and Further Resources

## Acknowledgment:

As I reflect on the journey of creating "Paris by Rail: A Travel Guide," I am filled with gratitude for the many individuals who have contributed their time, expertise, and support to bring this guide to life.

To the passionate team at Travel Guides Publishing, thank you for your unwavering dedication to crafting a comprehensive and insightful travel resource for exploring the enchanting city of Paris by rail. Your creativity, professionalism, and tireless efforts have truly made this project a reality.

I extend my deepest appreciation to the talented writers, researchers, and editors who have poured their hearts and souls into capturing the essence of Paris through vivid descriptions, practical tips, and insider recommendations. Your commitment to excellence and attention to detail have elevated this guide to a standard of excellence.

A special thank you to the residents of Paris who generously shared their local knowledge, hidden gems, and insider secrets to help us provide readers with an authentic and immersive travel experience. Your passion for your city has enriched the pages of this guide and will undoubtedly inspire countless rail travelers on their adventures in Paris.

I am grateful to the dedicated photographers and artists whose stunning images and illustrations have brought Paris to life within the pages of this guide. Your impactful visuals have captured the beauty, charm, and diversity of Paris, inviting readers to start on a visual journey alongside the written word.

To the travelers, explorers, and dreamers who seek adventure and discovery through the pages of "Paris by Rail: A Travel Guide," thank you for entrusting us to be your companion on this rail journey through the City of Light. May this guide spark your curiosity, ignite your sense of wonder, and help you create unforgettable memories in Paris.

Lastly, to my family, friends, and loved ones who have stood by me with unwavering support, encouragement, and understanding throughout the process of bringing this guide to fruition, your belief in me has been my greatest source of strength and inspiration. Thank you for being my guiding stars in this creative endeavor.

To everyone who has played a part in making "Paris by Rail: A Travel Guide" a reality, your contributions have not gone unnoticed or unappreciated. This guide is a testament to the collective effort, passion, and collaboration that have gone into celebrating the magic of Paris and the joy of rail travel.

With heartfelt thanks and warm wishes,

[Graham Vishai]

## Dedication:

To the wanderers, the dreamers, and the adventurers who find joy in the journey,
This book is dedicated to you.

May the gentle rhythm of the rails carry you through the heart of Paris,
Each journey a new chapter in your grand exploration.

May the sights, sounds, and scents of this enchanting city
Ignite your sense of wonder and ignite your spirit of adventure.

May the pages of this guide be your trusted companion,
Guiding you through the winding streets and grand boulevards of Paris.

For in the echoes of train whistles and the hum of passing landscapes,
There is magic to be found, stories waiting to unfold.

So, to all who commence on this rail journey through Paris,
May your travels be filled with discovery, delight, and moments of pure enchantment.

With love and wanderlust,
[Graham Vishai]

# Chapter 1 Introduction

## 1.1 Welcome to Paris by Rail

**Thank you for choosing "Paris by Rail" for your travel experience! Whether you are a seasoned traveler or kickstarting on your first European adventure, Paris by Rail offers an exciting and convenient way to explore the City of Light. Sit back, relax, and let the rhythmic sound of the train tracks carry you through the stunning landscapes of France to your destination – the magical city of Paris. From iconic landmarks to charming cafes, Paris has something for every traveler. Get ready to immerse yourself in the rich history, culture, and cuisine that make Paris a truly enchanting destination. So, welcome aboard, and let's begin your Parisian adventure by rail!**

## 1.2 Why Choose Rail Travel for Exploring Paris

Choosing rail travel for exploring Paris offers a unique and enriching experience that sets it apart from other modes of transportation. Here are some compelling reasons why rail travel is the ideal way to explore the City of Light:

1. Convenience: Paris boasts an extensive rail network that connects the city center to its surrounding suburbs and iconic landmarks. With numerous train stations conveniently located throughout the city, exploring Paris by rail allows for seamless travel between attractions, saving you time and hassle.

2. Efficiency: Trains in Paris are known for their punctuality and efficiency, making them a reliable mode of transportation for travelers. Whether you're heading to the Eiffel Tower, the Louvre, or Montmartre, you can count on the city's rail system to get you to your destination in a timely manner.

3. Scenic Routes: Rail travel offers a unique perspective of the French countryside as you journey towards Paris. Enjoy picturesque views of rolling hills, charming villages, and vineyards along the way,

adding an element of beauty and tranquility to your travel experience.

4. Cost-Effective: Compared to other transportation options, such as taxis or rental cars, rail travel in Paris can be a more budget-friendly choice for travelers looking to explore the city without breaking the bank. Additionally, booking in advance often allows for discounted fares, making it an affordable option for all budgets.

5. Environmental Sustainability: Opting for rail travel aligns with eco-conscious travel practices, as trains are a more sustainable mode of transportation compared to cars or planes. By choosing to explore Paris by rail, you are reducing your carbon footprint and contributing to a greener way of traveling.

6. Local Experience: Riding the rails in Paris offers a glimpse into the daily lives of locals as they commute to work, run errands, or simply enjoy the city. Immerse yourself in the bustling atmosphere of the train stations, strike up conversations with fellow passengers, and get a taste of authentic Parisian life along the way.

7. Accessibility: Parisian rail stations are designed to be accessible to all travelers, including those with

mobility concerns or special needs. Elevators, ramps, and other facilities are available to ensure a smooth and inclusive travel experience for everyone.

8. Flexibility: With frequent departures and various ticket options available, rail travel in Paris offers travelers the flexibility to craft their itinerary according to their preferences. Whether you're planning a day trip to Versailles or hopping between museums, the city's rail system provides the freedom to explore at your own pace.

In conclusion, choosing rail travel for exploring Paris not only offers practical advantages such as convenience and efficiency but also enhances your overall travel experience with scenic views, cost-effectiveness, sustainability, and a deeper connection to the local culture. So, hop aboard the next train and Start on a journey through the iconic streets of Paris – a city best explored by rail.

## 1.3 How to Use This Guide

To make the most of this guide for exploring Paris by rail, follow these simple steps:

1. Maneuver the pages: This guide is divided into various aspects of rail travel in Paris, including reasons to choose rail travel, tips for navigating the city's rail system, recommended destinations, and more. Scroll through the pages to find the information you need.

2. Plan Your Itinerary: Start by outlining your travel itinerary and identifying the key attractions you wish to visit in Paris. Consider how rail travel can help you reach these destinations efficiently and conveniently.

3. Learn About the Rail System: Familiarize yourself with the Parisian rail system, including the main train stations, types of trains available, ticketing options, and schedules. Understanding how the rail network operates will help you cruise the city with ease.

4. Check for Updates: Before your journey, check for any updates or changes to the train schedules or routes. Stay informed about any disruptions that may affect your travel plans and adjust accordingly.

5. Purchase Tickets: Determine the best ticket option for your travel needs, whether it's a single journey ticket, a multi-day pass, or a tourist package that

includes transportation and sightseeing activities. Purchase your tickets in advance to save time and money.

6. Pack Essentials: Pack essentials such as a map of the rail network, a travel card for easy access to stations, a water bottle, snacks, and any necessary travel documents. Dress comfortably and be prepared for different weather conditions.

7. Explore Recommended Destinations: Discover the must-see attractions and hidden gems in Paris that are easily accessible by rail. From iconic landmarks like the Eiffel Tower and Notre-Dame Cathedral to vibrant neighborhoods like Montmartre and Le Marais, explore a diverse range of destinations.

8. Immerse Yourself in Local Culture: Take advantage of the local experience that rail travel offers by interacting with fellow passengers, observing daily life in Paris, and sampling authentic cuisine at train station cafes and markets.

9. Stay Safe and Informed: Practice caution and adhere to safety guidelines while traveling on the Parisian rail system. Keep your belongings secure, be aware of your surroundings, and seek assistance from station staff or officials if needed.

**10. Enjoy the Journey:** Embrace the beauty and charm of Paris as you travel by rail through its enchanting landscapes and iconic landmarks. Take in the sights, sounds, and flavors of the city as you immerse yourself in a truly memorable travel experience.

By following these steps and using this guide as a resource, you can cruise Paris by rail with confidence and make the most of your travel adventures in the City of Light. Bon voyage!

## Chapter 2 Getting Ready

## 2.1 Planning Your Trip to Paris by Rail

Planning a trip to Paris by rail is an exciting adventure that offers convenience, efficiency, and a unique way to explore the City of Light. Here are some essential steps to help you plan your journey:

1. Set Your Travel Dates: Decide on your travel dates and the duration of your stay in Paris. Consider factors such as weather, special events, and peak tourist seasons when planning your trip.

2. Research Rail Options: Familiarize yourself with the different rail options available for traveling to and within Paris. Research high-speed trains, regional trains, metro systems, and other public transportation services to determine the best routes for your itinerary.

3. Choose Your Rail Pass: Depending on the length of your stay and your planned activities, consider whether a rail pass would be beneficial for your trip.

Look into options such as the Paris Visite Pass, Navigo Decouverte card, or single journey tickets based on your needs.

4. **Select Your Accommodation:** Choose accommodation that is conveniently located near a train station or metro stop to facilitate easy access to the city's transportation network. Consider factors such as budget, amenities, and proximity to tourist attractions.

5. **Create an Itinerary:** Plan your itinerary by outlining the attractions, neighborhoods, and experiences you wish to explore in Paris. Consider grouping activities by proximity to save time and maximize your sightseeing opportunities.

6. **Check Visa Requirements:** If you are traveling from abroad, ensure that you have the necessary visa and travel documents required to enter France. Check the visa requirements well in advance to avoid any last-minute complications.

7. **Pack Smartly:** Pack according to the season and activities you have planned in Paris. Include essentials like comfortable shoes for walking, travel adapters, a portable charger, a travel guidebook, and any specific items you may need for your journey.

8. Learn Basic French Phrases: Brush up on basic French phrases to help you cruise the city, interact with locals, and enhance your cultural experience. Simple greetings, directions, and food-related phrases can be especially useful.

9. Stay Informed: Stay updated on any travel advisories, transportation disruptions, or safety guidelines related to your trip. Check the weather forecast, transportation schedules, and any cultural events happening during your stay in Paris.

10. Stay Flexible: While planning is essential, remain open to unexpected discoveries and spontaneous detours during your trip. Allow yourself the flexibility to adjust your itinerary based on local recommendations and personal preferences.

By following these steps and preparing thoroughly for your trip to Paris by rail, you can set the stage for a memorable and enjoyable travel experience in one of the world's most enchanting cities. Bon voyage!

## 2.2 Choosing the Right Time to Visit

Choosing the right time to visit Paris can significantly impact your travel experience, considering factors like weather, crowds, and special events. Here are some key considerations to help you decide on the perfect time for your trip:

1. Weather: Paris experiences four distinct seasons, each offering a unique atmosphere. Spring (March to May) and fall (September to November) are popular seasons with mild temperatures and blooming gardens. Summer (June to August) can be warm and vibrant, ideal for outdoor activities. Winter (December to February) brings a festive ambiance but colder weather.

2. Peak Tourist Seasons: Peak tourist seasons in Paris are during the summer months, especially in July and August when many Europeans take their holidays. Spring and fall are also popular times, with increased crowds at major attractions and higher accommodation prices. Consider visiting during the shoulder seasons for fewer crowds and better deals.

3. Special Events: Check the Paris events calendar for festivals, exhibitions, and cultural events happening during your planned visit. Consider events like the Paris Fashion Week, Fête de la Musique, Bastille Day celebrations, and Christmas markets

when deciding on your travel dates for a unique experience.

**4. Budget:** Prices for accommodation, flights, and attractions can vary depending on the time of year. Traveling during the off-peak seasons or midweek can often lead to more affordable rates and better deals. Consider your budget and travel preferences when selecting the right time to visit Paris.

**5. Personal Preferences:** Take into account your personal preferences and interests when choosing the timing of your trip. If you enjoy outdoor activities and long days, summer might be the best choice. For a more relaxed experience with fewer crowds, consider visiting during the shoulder seasons.

**6. Transportation and Accommodation Availability:** Be mindful of transportation schedules and accommodation availability during peak seasons. Booking trains and accommodations in advance can help secure your preferred options and avoid last-minute inconveniences.

**7. Local Holidays and Closures:** Check for any local holidays, festivals, or closures that may affect your travel plans. Some attractions or shops may have altered hours during public holidays or special events, so plan accordingly to make the most of your visit.

8. **Weather Considerations:** Paris can be rainy throughout the year, so be prepared for unpredictable weather by packing layers, an umbrella, and comfortable shoes for walking. Check the weather forecast closer to your travel dates to pack accordingly.

9. **Crowd Avoidance:** If you prefer to explore Paris without large crowds, consider visiting early in the morning or later in the evening when popular attractions are less busy. Alternatively, explore off-the-beaten-path neighborhoods and hidden gems to escape the tourist crowds.

10. **Local Insights:** Seek recommendations from locals or experienced travelers on the best time to visit Paris based on your interests and preferences. Online travel forums, blogs, and social media platforms can provide valuable insights and insider tips for planning your trip.

Ultimately, the best time to visit Paris is a personal choice that depends on your preferences, budget, and travel goals. Whether you choose to experience the city's vibrant summer vibes, colorful fall foliage, festive winter markets, or blooming spring gardens, Paris offers something special year-round for every type of traveler.

## 2.3 Booking Rail Tickets and Passes

Booking rail tickets and passes for your upcoming travel can be a convenient and cost-effective way to explore different destinations. Here are some tips to help you maneuver the process:

**1. Plan Your Itinerary:** Before booking rail tickets or passes, plan your itinerary and decide on the destinations you want to visit. Consider the distances between cities, the frequency of train services, and any specific attractions or landmarks you want to see along the way.

**2. Choose the Right Rail Pass:** Depending on your travel preferences and itinerary, you can choose between individual point-to-point tickets or rail passes, such as Eurail or Interrail, which offer unlimited travel within a specific region or country for a set period. Compare the cost and coverage of different pass options to determine the best fit for your trip.

**3. Check Train Schedules:** Research the train schedules and frequencies for your chosen routes to ensure that you can travel comfortably and efficiently between destinations. Take note of any express or scenic train routes that you may want to experience during your journey.

**4. Book in Advance:** To secure the best prices and availability, consider booking your rail tickets or passes in advance. Many rail operators offer discounted fares for early bookings, especially for high-speed or long-distance trains.

**5. Consider Seat Reservations:** For certain train services, seat reservations may be required or recommended, especially during peak travel seasons or on popular routes. Check if your ticket or pass includes seat reservations or if you need to book them separately for a nominal fee.

**6. Check for Discounts:** Explore potential discounts for rail travel, such as youth, senior, or group fares, as well as special promotions or sales that may be available for certain routes or times of the year. Be sure to inquire about any available discounts when booking your tickets or passes.

7. **Travel During Off-Peak Hours:** Opting for off-peak travel times can not only save you money but also provide a more relaxed and less crowded journey. Consider traveling during weekdays or outside of rush hours to enjoy a more comfortable train experience.

8. **Understand Ticket Flexibility:** Different rail tickets and passes offer varying levels of flexibility in terms of travel dates, routes, and changes. Be aware of any restrictions or penalties associated with making changes to your booking and choose the option that best suits your travel plans.

9. **Validate Your Pass:** If you are using a rail pass, make sure to validate it before boarding your first train. Typically, this involves getting your pass stamped at a ticket counter or self-service kiosk at the train station to activate its validity for the duration of your trip.

10. **Manage Your Tickets:** Keep your rail tickets or passes in a safe place and easily accessible during your journey. Consider storing digital copies on your smartphone or tablet for convenient access and as a backup in case of loss or theft.

By following these tips and being proactive in planning and booking your rail tickets and passes, you can streamline your travel logistics and enjoy a seamless and memorable train journey through various destinations. Don't hesitate to reach out to rail operators or ticketing platforms for assistance with booking, route planning, or any inquiries related to your rail travel experience.

## 2.4 Currency and money matters

Understanding currency and money matters when visiting Paris is essential to ensure a smooth and hassle-free travel experience. Here are some key points to keep in mind:

1. Currency:
- The official currency of France is the Euro (€). It is denoted by the symbol € and is used throughout the country, including Paris. Make sure to familiarize yourself with Euro banknotes and coins to facilitate transactions.

2. Banknotes and Coins:
- Euro banknotes come in various denominations, including €5, €10, €20, €50, €100, €200, and €500.

Euro coins are available in denominations of 1 cent, 2 cents, 5 cents, 10 cents, 20 cents, 50 cents, €1, and €2.

3. Exchange Rates:
- Stay updated on the exchange rates between your home currency and the Euro to understand the value of your money while in Paris. Currency exchange services are available at airports, banks, exchange bureaus, and some hotels.

4. ATMs:
- ATMs, known as "Distributeurs Automatiques de Billets" (DAB) in French, are widely available throughout Paris. You can use your debit or credit card to withdraw cash in Euros. Be aware of any additional fees that your bank may charge for international transactions.

5. Credit Cards:
- Credit cards, such as Visa, MasterCard, and American Express, are widely accepted in Paris, especially in restaurants, hotels, shops, and tourist attractions. Notify your bank before traveling to ensure your card works seamlessly in France.

6. Cash vs. Card:
- While credit cards are commonly accepted, it's advisable to carry some cash for small purchases,

markets, and establishments that do not accept cards. Additionally, having cash on hand can be helpful in case of emergencies or when visiting rural areas.

7. Tipping:
- Tipping in Paris is not obligatory as a service charge is often included in the bill at restaurants and cafes. However, it is customary to round up the bill or leave a small gratuity for exceptional service. Tipping taxi drivers is also common, with a 10% tip considered appropriate.

8. VAT Refunds:
- When shopping in Paris, you may be eligible for a Value Added Tax (VAT) refund on certain purchases. Look for stores displaying a "Tax-Free Shopping" logo and request a tax refund form. Remember to present the form and your purchases at the airport for a VAT refund before leaving the EU.

9. Budgeting:
- Plan your budget accordingly for your trip to Paris, considering expenses such as accommodation, meals, transportation, sightseeing, and shopping. Keep track of your spending to ensure you stay within your budget and avoid unnecessary expenses.

10. Currency Exchange:

- If you need to exchange currency, compare rates at different exchange bureaus to get the best deal. Avoid exchanging money at airports or tourist hotspots, as they typically offer less favorable rates. It's recommended to use ATMs for cash withdrawals or pay by card whenever possible.

11. Shopping and Bargaining:
- When shopping in markets or smaller stores, bargaining is not common practice in Paris. Prices are generally fixed, especially in established retail outlets. However, you may negotiate prices at flea markets or when purchasing multiple items.

12. Safety and Security:
- Be cautious when carrying cash or using ATMs in crowded areas to prevent theft or fraud. Keep your valuables secure and use ATMs located in well-lit, secure locations. Notify your bank immediately if your card is lost or stolen.

By understanding these currency and money matters in Paris, you can manage your finances effectively, make informed decisions about payments, and enjoy a seamless travel experience in the French capital.

## 2.5 Packing Tips for Rail Travel

Packing for a rail travel adventure requires thoughtful consideration to ensure you have everything you need for a comfortable and convenient journey. Here are some packing tips to help you prepare for your next train trip:

**1. Pack Light:** Rail travel typically involves moving between stations and possibly carrying your belongings up and down stairs or through crowded platforms. Opt for a lightweight and easy-to-carry luggage or backpack to make your journey more manageable.

**2. Check Baggage Allowances:** Before packing, familiarize yourself with the baggage allowances and restrictions of the rail service you'll be using. Ensure that your luggage complies with size and weight requirements to avoid any potential issues during your journey.

**3. Organize Essentials:** Pack essential items such as travel documents, identification, tickets or passes, money, credit cards, and a copy of your itinerary in a secure and easily accessible place. Consider using a travel organizer or document holder to keep everything in one place.

4. Clothing Selection: Pack versatile and comfortable clothing suitable for the climate and activities at your destination. Consider layers that can be easily added or removed to adjust to changing temperatures. Include a mix of casual and smart attire for various occasions.

5. Footwear: Choose comfortable and sturdy footwear for walking and exploring new destinations. Opt for shoes that provide good support and are easy to slip on and off, especially if you'll be passing through security checks at train stations.

6. Travel Accessories: Don't forget to pack travel accessories such as a travel pillow, eye mask, earplugs, charger and adapter for electronic devices, reusable water bottle, snacks, entertainment (books, magazines, music), and any medications or personal care items you may need during your journey.

7. Pack Snacks and Refreshments: While many trains offer dining options onboard, it's always a good idea to pack some snacks and refreshments to keep you fueled and hydrated throughout your journey. Choose non-perishable and easy-to-carry items to enjoy on the go.

**8. Entertainment:** Long train journeys provide the perfect opportunity to relax and indulge in some entertainment. Pack a book, e-reader, tablet, or download movies or podcasts to keep yourself entertained during the trip. Don't forget headphones for a more immersive experience.

**9. Travel Comfort Items:** Consider packing travel comfort items such as a small blanket, travel pillow, eye mask, and earplugs to help you relax and rest during your journey, especially if you'll be traveling overnight or for long hours.

**10. First Aid Kit:** It's always wise to have a basic first aid kit with essentials such as bandages, pain relievers, motion sickness medication, insect repellent, and any specific medication you may need. Be prepared for minor health concerns that may arise during your trip.

**11. Security Measures:** Ensure that your luggage is secure and easily identifiable by using luggage tags with your contact information. Consider packing a small lock for added security, especially if you'll be leaving your luggage unattended during stopovers.

**12. Check Local Customs:** If you'll be traveling to different regions or countries, research and adhere to any specific cultural norms or dress codes to ensure that your clothing and belongings are respectful and appropriate for your destinations.

By packing thoughtfully and efficiently for your rail travel adventure, you can focus on enjoying the journey and exploring new destinations without the burden of carrying unnecessary items or facing packing-related challenges along the way. Don't hesitate to customize your packing list based on your personal preferences, travel style, and destination requirements to make your train journey a seamless and enjoyable experience.

## Chapter 3 Arriving in Paris

## 3.1 Arriving at Gare du Nord: Your Gateway to Paris

Arriving at Gare du Nord, one of Paris' busiest train stations, marks the beginning of your journey in the enchanting city of lights. Here are some tips to help you maneuver your arrival at Gare du Nord and make the most of your time in Paris:

1. Orientation: Take a moment to familiarize yourself with the layout of Gare du Nord. The station can be bustling with activity, so it's helpful to know where the main exits, ticket counters, information desks, and transportation options are located.

2. Transportation Options: From Gare du Nord, you can easily access various transportation options to reach your accommodation or explore the city. The station is well-connected with metro lines, buses, taxis, and even bike-sharing services. Consider purchasing a Paris Visite pass for unlimited travel on public transportation during your stay.

3. Language: While English is widely spoken in tourist areas, learning a few basic French phrases can be helpful and appreciated by locals. Don't be afraid to engage with locals in French, as it can enhance your cultural experience in Paris.

4. Currency Exchange: If you need to exchange currency upon arrival, Gare du Nord offers currency exchange services or ATMs where you can withdraw Euros. Be mindful of exchange rates and fees when conducting currency transactions.

5. Luggage Storage: If you arrive in Paris early or have some time before check-in at your accommodation, you can utilize luggage storage services available at Gare du Nord. This allows you to explore the city unencumbered by your bags.

6. Information Desks: If you have any questions or need assistance, don't hesitate to approach the information desks at Gare du Nord. The staff can provide directions, maps, transportation information, and recommendations for your stay in Paris.

7. Connecting to Other Stations: If you have connecting trains at other Parisian stations such as Gare de l'Est or Gare Saint-Lazare, familiarize yourself with the transportation options to seamlessly transfer between stations. Paris has an extensive public transportation network that can take you to various parts of the city quickly and efficiently.

8. Nearby Attractions: Gare du Nord is located in the 10th arrondissement of Paris, close to popular attractions such as Montmartre, the Sacré-Cœur Basilica, and the Canal Saint-Martin. Consider exploring these nearby attractions after your arrival or before departing from Paris.

**9. Safety Tips:** As with any travel destination, stay vigilant about your belongings and surroundings while in transit and at train stations. Keep your valuables secure and be mindful of pickpockets in crowded areas.

**10. Accommodation:** If you haven't already booked accommodation in Paris, Gare du Nord is well-connected to various neighborhoods with a range of hotels, hostels, and vacation rentals. Consider the proximity to public transportation and main attractions when selecting your lodging.

**11. Dining Options:** Whether you're looking for a quick bite or a sit-down meal, Gare du Nord offers a variety of dining options including cafés, bakeries, and restaurants. Treat yourself to a croissant or a café au lait to kick off your Parisian experience.

**12. Local Etiquette:** Familiarize yourself with local customs and etiquette in Paris, such as greeting others with a polite "bonjour," respecting meal times, and adopting a relaxed pace to savor the beauty of the city.

Embrace the charm and elegance of Paris as you step out of Gare du Nord and into the heart of the French capital. Enjoy the iconic landmarks, delicious cuisine, and rich culture that make Paris a timeless destination for travelers from around the world. Bon voyage et profitez de votre séjour à Paris! (Safe travels and enjoy your stay in Paris!)

## 3.2 How to arrive in Paris via train from any part of the world

Arriving in Paris by train is a convenient and scenic way to start your journey in the city of lights. Here are some general steps to help you arrive in Paris via train from any part of the world:

1. Choose Your Route: Research and select a train route that connects your location to Paris. Depending on your starting point, you may need to take multiple trains or transfer at different stations along the way. Popular international train routes to Paris include the Eurostar from London, Thalys from Brussels or Amsterdam, and TGV from cities across Europe.

2. Book Your Tickets: Purchase your train tickets in advance through the train operator's website, a ticketing agency, or at the train station. Consider booking flexible tickets if you anticipate changes in your travel plans. It's advisable to book tickets early

to secure seat reservations, especially during peak travel seasons.

3. **Check Visa Requirements:** Make sure you have the necessary visas and travel documents to enter France if you are traveling from a country outside the Schengen Area. Verify the visa requirements based on your nationality and the duration of your stay in Paris.

4. **Pack Essentials:** Pack your travel essentials including your passport, tickets, visa documents, comfortable clothing, travel adapters, medications, and any other items you may need during your journey. Consider packing light to make it easier to cruise train stations and platforms.

5. **Plan Your Itinerary:** Familiarize yourself with the train schedule, station stops, and transfer points along your route to Paris. Create a rough itinerary of your journey including estimated arrival times, connecting trains, and any layovers you may have.

6. **Arrive at the Train Station:** Arrive at the train station well in advance of your departure time to allow for ticket validation, security checks, and boarding procedures. Follow the signs to locate your

platform and train carriage based on your ticket information.

**7. Board the Train:** Once your train arrives, board the train and find your seat or assigned compartment. Store your luggage in the designated areas and settle in for your journey to Paris.

**8. Enjoy the Ride:** Sit back, relax, and enjoy the scenic views as you travel to Paris by train. Admire the passing landscapes, quaint villages, and iconic landmarks along the way. Consider bringing a book, music, or snacks to make your journey more comfortable.

**9. Prepare for Arrival:** As you approach Paris, gather your belongings and prepare to disembark at your designated station. Keep your ticket handy as you may need it to exit the station or pass through ticket gates.

**10. Exit the Station:** Upon arrival in Paris, follow the signs to exit the train station and enter the city. Take a moment to orient yourself with your surroundings and review your transportation options to reach your accommodation or explore the city.

11. Explore Paris: Once you've arrived in Paris, immerse yourself in the charm and beauty of the city. Visit iconic landmarks such as the Eiffel Tower, Louvre Museum, Notre-Dame Cathedral, and Montmartre. Indulge in Parisian cuisine, stroll along the Seine River, and soak up the vibrant atmosphere of the neighborhoods.

Arriving in Paris by train offers a unique and memorable experience that allows you to witness the changing landscapes of Europe as you journey to the heart of the French capital. Embrace the romance and allure of train travel as you commence on your Parisian adventure. Bon voyage et profitez de votre séjour à Paris! (Safe travels and enjoy your stay in Paris!)

## 3.3 Navigating the Train Station

Navigating the train station in Paris, such as Gare du Nord or Gare de Lyon, can be a bustling experience due to the size and volume of travelers. Here are some tips specifically tailored for navigating train stations in Paris:

1. Arrival: Upon arrival at the Paris train station, take a moment to absorb the hustle and bustle

around you. Look for signs in French and English indicating the different facilities and services available within the station.

2. Ticket Validation: Ensure your ticket is validated before boarding the train. Make sure to familiarize yourself with the different types of ticket validation machines used in Paris train stations to avoid any issues during your journey.

3. Information Desks: Head to the information desks located within the train station if you need assistance with directions, train schedules, or any other inquiries. The staff at the information desks are usually multilingual and can assist you in English.

4. Metro Connections: Some Paris train stations, like Gare du Nord, have direct connections to the Paris Metro system. Look for signs indicating the Metro entrances within the station if you need to transfer to the Metro for your onward journey.

5. Signage: Pay close attention to the signage in the train station, which will guide you to platforms, ticket counters, restrooms, exits, and other facilities. The signs in Paris train stations are usually well-marked but can sometimes be overwhelming due to the station's size.

**6. Security Checks:** Be prepared to undergo security checks before entering the platforms. Keep your ticket and identification handy for inspection, and follow the instructions of security personnel to ensure a smooth passage through the security checkpoint.

**7. Thalys and Eurostar:** If you are traveling on international high-speed trains like Thalys or Eurostar, make sure to arrive at the station well in advance to complete passport control and security checks before boarding your train.

**8. Concourse Areas:** Cruise through the station's concourse areas to locate amenities such as cafes, shops, restrooms, and waiting areas. Take note of the location of these facilities to make your wait more comfortable before boarding your train.

**9. Multilingual Assistance:** If you have trouble understanding the signage or announcements in French, look for information in English or ask station staff for assistance. Many staff members at Paris train stations speak English and can help you with any language barriers.

**10. RER Connections:** Some Paris train stations, like Gare de Lyon, also serve as hubs for the RER

(Regional Express Network) trains. If you need to transfer to an RER train for suburban travel, follow the signs indicating RER connections within the station.

**11. Boarding Procedures:** Follow the boarding procedures for your specific train, including checking your platform number, waiting in the designated area, and boarding the train only when permitted. Be mindful of any announcements regarding your train departure.

**12. Taxi and Transportation:** If you need to take a taxi or other transportation from the train station, follow the signs to the designated taxi stands or transportation hubs outside the station. Avoid soliciting services from unauthorized individuals.

**13. Luggage Assistance:** If you have heavy luggage or belongings, consider using trolleys or luggage carts available at the train station to transport your items to the platforms or waiting areas. Be cautious of your belongings at all times to prevent theft or loss.

**14. Wi-Fi and Charging Stations:** Some Paris train stations offer Wi-Fi services and charging stations for travelers. Look for information about these amenities to stay connected and charged while waiting for your train.

**15. Relaxation Areas:** If you have time before your train departs, consider exploring relaxation areas or lounges within the train station where you can unwind and wait comfortably. Some stations may offer seating areas, cafes, or designated waiting zones.

By keeping these tips in mind and staying alert while navigating the train stations in Paris, you can efficiently cruise the bustling terminals and enjoy a seamless travel experience during your time in the City of Light.

## 3.4 Connecting to the Metro and Other Public Transport

Connecting to the Metro and other public transport options in Paris is a convenient and efficient way to explore the city beyond the train stations. Here are some tips to help you maneuver the Metro and public transportation network in Paris:

**1. Metro Map:** Familiarize yourself with the Paris Metro map, which consists of 16 lines that cover the entire city and its suburbs. The Metro is color-coded and numbered, making it easy to maneuver once you understand the system.

2. Ticket Options: Purchase Metro tickets or passes at ticket machines or counters within the train stations or Metro stations. Options include single-use tickets, carnet (pack of 10 tickets), and day passes for unlimited travel within certain zones.

3. Transfers: When transferring between Metro lines or to other modes of public transport like buses or trams, look for signs indicating connections within the stations. Follow the directions to the appropriate platform or stop for your desired destination.

4. RER Trains: The RER (Regional Express Network) trains connect Paris to its suburbs and surrounding areas. Some RER stations are integrated with the Metro system, while others require separate tickets. Pay attention to RER signage and ticket requirements for your journey.

5. Bus Stops: Explore Paris by bus by locating bus stops near Metro stations or popular attractions. Bus routes cover areas not serviced by the Metro and provide a scenic way to see the city. Check bus

schedules and routes in advance for a smoother journey.

**6. NFC Technology:** Consider using NFC technology on your smartphone for contactless payments on public transport in Paris. Many Metro stations and buses accept contactless payment methods for added convenience during your travels.

**7. Night Transport:** Plan your nighttime travels using the Noctilien night bus network, which operates after the Metro and regular buses have stopped running. Noctilien buses cover various routes throughout the city and its suburbs, providing a safe transport option late at night.

**8. Velib Bike Share:** Embrace a greener way to explore Paris by utilizing the Velib bike-share system. Rent a bike from one of the many stations around the city and enjoy cycling along designated paths and lanes to reach your destinations.

**9. Navigo Card:** Consider purchasing a Navigo card if you plan to use public transport frequently during your stay in Paris. The Navigo card offers unlimited travel within certain zones and can be a cost-effective option for visitors staying longer in the city.

10. Elevators and Accessibility: If you require accessibility options, look for stations with elevators or ramps for easy access to platforms and vehicles. Some Metro stations are equipped with facilities to accommodate passengers with mobility limitations.

11. Real-time Information: Stay informed about Metro and bus schedules, delays, and service updates by checking real-time information displays at stations or using mobile apps provided by the Paris public transport system. These tools can help you plan your journeys effectively.

12. Common Courtesy: When using public transport in Paris, practice common courtesy by giving up seats to those in need, respecting personal space, and following etiquette guidelines. Be mindful of other passengers and maintain a pleasant atmosphere during your travels.

13. Cultural Immersion: Use public transport in Paris as an opportunity to immerse yourself in the local culture and daily life of the city. Observing how Parisians maneuver the Metro and buses can provide insights into the rhythm and vibrancy of urban life in Paris.

14. Safety Tips: Stay vigilant while using public transport, especially during peak hours or in crowded areas. Keep your belongings secure, be aware of your surroundings, and report any suspicious behavior to authorities or transport staff.

By following these tips and recommendations, you can cruise the Metro and other public transport options in Paris with confidence and ease, allowing you to discover the diverse neighborhoods, iconic landmarks, and hidden gems that make the City of Light a captivating destination for visitors from around the world.

# Chapter 4 Exploring Paris by Rail

## 4.1 Understanding Parisian Rail Network

Exploring Paris by rail is a convenient and efficient way to maneuver the city and its surrounding areas. The Parisian rail network consists of the Metro, RER (Regional Express Network), and SNCF trains, providing comprehensive coverage and connectivity for residents and visitors alike. Here's a guide to help you understand and make the most of the rail network in Paris:

1. Paris Metro:
- The Paris Metro is the rapid transit system serving the city of Paris and its suburbs.
- It consists of 16 lines identified by numbers and colors, making it easy to navigate.
- The Metro operates from early morning until late at night, with frequent trains running at regular intervals.
- Metro stations are located throughout the city, allowing access to popular attractions, neighborhoods, and transportation hubs.

2. RER (Regional Express Network):
- The RER is a commuter rail system that connects Paris to its suburbs and nearby areas.
- RER trains are identified by letters (A, B, C, D, E) and colors, with each line serving specific destinations.
- Some RER stations are underground and integrated with the Metro system, while others are above ground.
- RER trains run less frequently than the Metro but cover longer distances, making them ideal for traveling to locations outside the city center.

3. SNCF Trains:
- The SNCF (French national railway company) operates regional and intercity trains connecting Paris to other regions in France and neighboring countries.
- Different types of SNCF trains, such as TGV (high-speed trains), TER (regional trains), and Intercités, offer varying levels of speed and comfort for long-distance travel.
- Paris is served by several major train stations, including Gare du Nord, Gare de l'Est, Gare de Lyon, Gare Montparnasse, Gare d'Austerlitz, and Gare Saint-Lazare, each offering connections to different parts of France and Europe.

**4. Interchange Stations:**
- Certain train stations in Paris serve as interchange points between the Metro, RER, and SNCF trains, providing seamless transfers for passengers.
- Pay attention to signage and announcements within stations to maneuver between different rail networks effectively.
- Interchange stations like Châtelet-Les Halles, Gare du Nord, and Saint-Michel-Notre-Dame are key hubs for transferring between different modes of transport.

**5. Ticketing:**
- Purchase tickets or passes for the Metro, RER, and SNCF trains at ticket machines or counters located within train stations or Metro stations.
- Options include single-use tickets, multi-ride passes (carnet), unlimited travel passes for certain zones, and discounted fares for seniors, students, and children.
- Validate your ticket before boarding the train or Metro by using the electronic validation machines located on platforms.

**6. Zones:**
- The Parisian rail network is divided into zones, with central Paris (Zone 1) encompassing popular areas

like the Champs-Élysées, Louvre Museum, and Eiffel Tower.
- Consider the zone coverage of your ticket or pass when planning your journeys, as some attractions and suburbs may fall outside Zone 1.

7. Timetables and Frequency:
- Check timetables for the Metro, RER, and SNCF trains to plan your journeys in advance.
- While the Metro and RER operate frequently during the day, SNCF train schedules may vary based on the destination and type of service.
- Be aware of any schedule changes due to holidays, strikes, or maintenance work that may affect your travel plans.

8. Accessibility:
- Many train stations in Paris are equipped with elevators, escalators, and ramps to accommodate passengers with reduced mobility or disabilities.
- Look for accessibility symbols or inquire at information desks for assistance in navigating stations and trains.

9. Travel Apps:
- Use mobile apps provided by the Paris public transport system, such as RATP and SNCF, to access

real-time information, plan routes, and receive updates on disruptions or delays.
- These apps can help you cruise the rail network more efficiently and make informed decisions while traveling in Paris.

10. Safety and Security:
- Maintain awareness of your surroundings while traveling on trains and in stations, especially during peak hours or in crowded areas.
- Keep your belongings secure, watch out for pickpockets, and report any suspicious behavior to authorities or railway staff.

By understanding the Parisian rail network and following these tips, you can confidently explore the city and its outskirts by train, immersing yourself in the rich culture, history, and vibrant atmosphere that Paris has to offer. Enjoy your rail adventures in the City of Light!

## 4.2 Overview of RER, Metro, and Tram Systems

The RER, Metro, and Tram systems are important modes of public transportation in various cities across the world. Each system serves to transport people efficiently within urban areas, offering different advantages and characteristics to cater to diverse transportation needs.

1. RER (Réseau Express Régional):
- Location: The RER system is primarily found in the Île-de-France region, specifically in Paris, France.
- Integration: The RER system is a regional commuter rail system that serves both the city center and the outskirts, connecting various suburbs with the heart of the city.
- Network: The RER network consists of five lines (A, B, C, D, and E), with each line covering specific routes and serving different areas within the region.
- Interconnectivity: The RER system is known for its integration with other modes of transportation, such as the Paris Metro, buses, and trams, providing passengers with seamless connections across different travel routes.
- Capacity: The RER trains are designed to accommodate a large number of passengers, making it a popular choice for daily commuters and travelers within the region.

2. Metro:
- Location: Metro systems can be found in major cities worldwide, including Paris, New York City, Tokyo, London, and many others.

- Underground Networks: Metro systems are typically underground or elevated, consisting of multiple lines that crisscross the city and provide access to various neighborhoods and landmarks.
- Rapid Transit: Metro trains offer high-frequency services, allowing passengers to travel quickly between stations within urban areas.
- Accessibility: Metro systems are known for their accessibility and convenience, with stations located at key points of interest, such as commercial areas, tourist attractions, and residential neighborhoods.
- Capacity: Metro trains are designed to carry a large number of passengers during peak hours, helping to alleviate traffic congestion and reduce reliance on private vehicles.

3. Tram:
- Location: Tram systems can be found in cities across Europe, Asia, and other parts of the world, offering localized transportation options within urban areas.
- Surface Transportation: Trams operate on tracks laid on the street, providing a convenient and environmentally friendly mode of transportation for short to medium-distance travel.
- Integration: Tram networks often complement metro and bus systems, serving as feeder lines that

connect neighborhoods and areas not easily accessible by other modes of transportation.
- Scenic Routes: Trams are popular for their scenic routes that often pass through historic districts, picturesque neighborhoods, and culturally significant areas, offering passengers a unique and enjoyable travel experience.
- Capacity: Trams are usually designed to carry a moderate number of passengers, making them suitable for shorter journeys within city limits.

In conclusion, the RER, Metro, and Tram systems play crucial roles in facilitating urban mobility and providing residents and visitors with efficient, reliable, and sustainable transportation options. Each system offers unique features and benefits tailored to the specific needs of different cities and regions, contributing to the overall accessibility and connectivity of urban areas around the world.

## 4.3 Types of Tickets and Passes

Tickets and passes are essential for using public transportation efficiently and conveniently. Depending on the city and the transportation system, various types of tickets and passes are available to cater to different needs of passengers. Here are some common types of tickets and passes that are often offered:

1. Single Ride Ticket:
- This ticket allows passengers to take a single journey on a specific mode of transportation, such as a bus, metro, tram, or train.
- It is usually valid for a limited time period after validation and is ideal for occasional travelers or those making a one-time trip.

2. Day Pass:
- A day pass offers unlimited travel on public transportation within a specific period, typically for 24 hours from the time of first use.
- This pass is suitable for tourists or passengers who plan to make multiple trips in a day and want to avoid the hassle of purchasing separate tickets for each journey.

3. Weekly/Monthly Pass:
- Weekly or monthly passes provide unlimited travel on public transportation for a longer duration, usually valid for 7 days (weekly) or a calendar month.
- These passes are popular among daily commuters and regular users of public transportation, offering

cost savings compared to purchasing individual tickets every day.

**4. Integrated Passes:**
- Integrated passes allow passengers to use multiple modes of transportation within a city or region, such as buses, metro, trams, and trains, using a single ticket or pass.
- These passes promote seamless travel and interconnectivity between different modes of transportation, enhancing the overall public transportation experience.

**5. Smart Cards or RFID Cards:**
- Smart cards or RFID cards are reloadable electronic cards that passengers can use to pay for public transportation fares.
- These cards offer convenience, speed, and contactless payment options, reducing the need for physical tickets or cash transactions.

**6. Group Passes:**
- Group passes are designed for multiple passengers traveling together, offering discounted fares or special rates for groups of a certain size.
- These passes are ideal for families, friends, or organized groups exploring a city together and can help reduce overall travel costs for the group.

## 7. Tourist Passes:
- Tourist passes are tailored for visitors exploring a city or region, providing unlimited travel on public transportation along with discounts or free entry to tourist attractions, museums, and other landmarks.
- These passes are convenient for tourists looking to maximize their sightseeing while enjoying hassle-free transportation options.

## 8. Senior/Youth Passes:
- Senior or youth passes offer discounted fares or special rates for older adults or young passengers, providing them with cost-effective transportation options.
- These passes cater to specific age groups and help make public transportation more accessible and affordable for seniors and youth.

Overall, the variety of tickets and passes available for public transportation systems aim to accommodate the diverse needs of passengers, whether they are daily commuters, tourists, groups, seniors, or youth. By choosing the most suitable ticket or pass based on their travel requirements, passengers can enjoy a seamless and efficient journey while exploring and navigating cities around the world.

## 4.4 Tips for Navigating Parisian Rail System

Navigating the Parisian rail system, which includes the metro, RER (Réseau Express Régional), and buses, can seem daunting at first but with a few tips and tricks, you can easily get around the city like a pro:

**1. Obtain a Map:** Before starting your journey, get a map of the Paris metro and RER system. You can find these maps at metro stations, tourist information centers, or download them online. Familiarize yourself with the different lines, connections, and key stations.

**2. Purchase the Right Ticket:** Decide on the type of ticket or pass that best suits your travel needs. Consider factors such as the duration of your stay, the frequency of travel, and the zones you will be traveling to and from. Single-use tickets, day passes, and multi-day passes are available for purchase.

**3. Validate Your Ticket:** If you are using a paper ticket, make sure to validate it before entering the metro or RER platform. Insert your ticket into the validation machine to imprint the date and time on it.

Skip this step if you are using a contactless card or pass.

4. **Mind the Direction:** Pay attention to the direction in which the train or metro is heading. Signs on the platform indicate the next train's destination and its terminus. Make sure you are boarding the correct train going in the right direction to avoid unnecessary detours.

5. **Transfer Points:** Some stations in Paris serve multiple metro lines or connect to the RER. Take note of these transfer points, as changing lines may require navigating underground passages or using stairs/elevators. Follow the signs for your transfer connection.

6. **Peak Hours Avoidance:** To minimize crowds and congestion, try to avoid traveling during peak hours in the morning and evening when commuters rush to and from work. Plan your trips earlier or later if possible to ensure a more comfortable journey.

7. **Accessibility Needs:** If you have accessibility needs or are traveling with bulky luggage, check for stations that have elevators or escalators. Not all stations in Paris are equipped with these facilities, so plan your route accordingly.

**8. Stay Alert:** Keep your belongings secure and be vigilant while traveling on public transport, especially during busy periods. Watch out for pickpockets and be cautious with your valuables.

**9. Use Official Apps:** Consider downloading official apps like RATP (Régie Autonome des Transports Parisiens) or Citymapper, which provide real-time information on routes, schedules, delays, and station updates. These apps can be invaluable for navigating the Parisian transport system.

**10. Learn Basic Phrases:** While most signage in Parisian transport systems is in French, you can often find English translations as well. Still, learning some basic French phrases related to transportation can be helpful, especially when interacting with staff or asking for directions.

By following these tips and familiarizing yourself with the Parisian rail system, you can cruise the city with ease and confidence. Embrace the efficiency and convenience of public transportation in Paris to explore all the iconic landmarks, neighborhoods, and cultural treasures the city has to offer.

# Chapter 5 Must-Visit Landmarks and Attractions

## 5.1 Eiffel Tower

The Eiffel Tower is an iconic symbol of Paris and a must-visit landmark for any visitor to the city. Standing at 324 meters tall, this wrought-iron lattice tower offers breathtaking views of Paris from its observation decks. Whether you choose to admire it from the Champ de Mars park or ascend to the top for panoramic views, the Eiffel Tower is a timeless symbol of romance and elegance in the heart of the city. Be sure to visit both during the day and at night when the tower is beautifully illuminated, creating a magical atmosphere.

To visit the Eiffel Tower by rail, you can use the Parisian metro or RER system. The Eiffel Tower is conveniently located near various metro and RER stations, making it easily accessible from different parts of the city. Here are the recommended routes to reach the Eiffel Tower by rail:

1. Metro: Take the metro Line 6 (green line) to the station "Bir-Hakeim" or Line 8 (pink line) to the station "École Militaire." Both stations are within walking distance to the Eiffel Tower. From there, follow the signs or the direction of the tower to reach your destination.

2. RER: If you are traveling from a location outside the city center, you can use the RER C line to reach the Eiffel Tower. Get off at the station "Champ de Mars - Tour Eiffel," which is the closest RER station to the Eiffel Tower. Follow the signs leading to the tower from the station.

By using the metro or RER system to access the Eiffel Tower, you can enjoy the convenience of public transportation and easily maneuver your way to this iconic Parisian landmark.

## 5.2 Louvre Museum

The Louvre Museum is one of the world's largest and most famous museums, home to thousands of works of art and historical artifacts spanning centuries. Located in the heart of Paris, the Louvre is a must-visit attraction for art and history lovers. Here is a glimpse into what makes the Louvre Museum a captivating destination:

1. Mona Lisa: One of the most famous artworks in the world, Leonardo da Vinci's "Mona Lisa" is housed in the Louvre. Visitors from all over the globe flock to see this enigmatic masterpiece up close.

2. Glass Pyramid: The modern glass pyramid entrance designed by architect I.M. Pei serves as the main entrance to the museum and has become an iconic part of the Louvre's architecture.

3. Art Collections: The Louvre's vast collection includes a diverse range of art forms, from ancient Egyptian artifacts to renowned paintings like the "Venus de Milo" and the "Winged Victory of Samothrace."

To visit the Louvre Museum by rail, you can utilize the efficient Parisian metro system. The museum is conveniently located near the Palais Royal - Musée du Louvre metro station, which provides easy access to this cultural gem. Here's the recommended route to reach the Louvre Museum by rail:

1. Metro: Take the metro Line 1 (yellow line) and alight at the "Palais Royal - Musée du Louvre"

station. This station is directly connected to the Louvre Museum, making it a convenient starting point for your visit.

Once you arrive at the Palais Royal - Musée du Louvre metro station, you can follow the signs or ask for directions to the museum entrance. The Louvre's iconic glass pyramid, designed by architect I.M. Pei, serves as the main entrance and is easily visible from the station.

By using the metro system and following this route, you can seamlessly reach the Louvre Museum and immerse yourself in its world-renowned art collections and historical treasures. Enjoy exploring one of the most famous museums in the world and make the most of your visit to this cultural masterpiece.

## 5.3 Notre-Dame Cathedral

To visit Notre-Dame Cathedral by rail, you can use the Parisian metro system. Before the tragic fire in 2019, Notre-Dame Cathedral was a beloved landmark in Paris, known for its stunning Gothic architecture and historical significance. While the cathedral is currently undergoing restoration, it remains an important symbol of Parisian history and resilience. Here's how you can reach Notre-Dame Cathedral by rail:

**1. Metro:** Take the metro Line 4 (light pink line) or Line 1 (yellow line) and alight at the "Cité" or "Saint-Michel - Notre-Dame" stations. Both stations are in close proximity to Notre-Dame Cathedral, allowing for easy access to this iconic monument.

Once you arrive at the Cité or Saint-Michel - Notre-Dame metro stations, simply follow the signs or inquire about the directions to Notre-Dame Cathedral. Despite the ongoing renovations, the exterior of the cathedral remains a sight to behold, with intricate stone carvings and majestic spires that reflect centuries of history and craftsmanship.

Visiting Notre-Dame Cathedral by rail offers a convenient and efficient way to experience the beauty and grandeur of this historic landmark. While the interior of the cathedral may not be fully accessible at this time, the exterior and surrounding area still provide a glimpse into the cultural significance of Notre-Dame Cathedral in Paris.

## 5.4 Champs-Élysées

To visit the Champs-Élysées by rail, you can make use of the Parisian metro system. The Champs-Élysées is one of the most famous avenues in the world, lined with shops, cafes, theaters, and iconic landmarks. Whether you want to stroll down the avenue, shop at luxury boutiques, or admire historic sites, the Champs-Élysées offers a vibrant and bustling atmosphere. Here's how you can reach the Champs-Élysées by rail:

1. Metro: Take the metro Line 1 (yellow line) and alight at either the "Champs-Élysées - Clemenceau" or "Franklin D. Roosevelt" station. Both stations provide convenient access to different sections of the Champs-Élysées avenue.

Once you arrive at the Champs-Élysées - Clemenceau or Franklin D. Roosevelt metro stations, you can easily explore the avenue on foot. From the Arc de Triomphe at one end to the Place de la Concorde at the other, the Champs-Élysées offers a mix of grand architecture, designer boutiques, cafes, and cultural attractions.

By taking the metro and following this route, you can immerse yourself in the vibrant atmosphere of the

Champs-Élysées and enjoy everything this iconic avenue has to offer. Whether you're interested in shopping, dining, or simply soaking in the Parisian ambiance, the Champs-Élysées is a must-visit destination that captures the essence of Paris in all its splendor.

## 5.5 Montmartre

To visit Montmartre by rail, you can use the Parisian metro system, which provides easy access to this charming neighborhood known for its artistic heritage, picturesque streets, and the iconic Sacré-Cœur Basilica. Here's how you can reach Montmartre by rail:

1. Metro: Take the metro Line 2 (blue line) and alight at the "Anvers" or "Pigalle" station. Both stations are conveniently located near Montmartre and offer access to different parts of this historic neighborhood.

Upon arriving at the Anvers or Pigalle metro station, you can start your exploration of Montmartre on foot. Wander through the winding cobblestone streets, admire the vibrant street art, and soak in the bohemian atmosphere that has inspired generations of artists.

Montmartre is also home to the majestic Sacré-Cœur Basilica, located at the summit of the hill. You can climb the stairs or take the funicular to reach the basilica and enjoy panoramic views of Paris from the domed terrace.

By taking the metro and following this route, you can discover the artistic and cultural richness of Montmartre, from the bustling Place du Tertre to the tranquil Vineyard of Montmartre. Immerse yourself in the history and charm of this unique neighborhood and experience the romantic allure that has captivated visitors for centuries.

## 5.6 Seine River Cruise

To enjoy a Seine River cruise, you have several options for boarding points along the riverbanks in Paris, where you can relax and take in the iconic sights of the city from a unique perspective on the water. Here's how you can cruise on a Seine River cruise:

**1. Batobus:** Batobus is a hop-on-hop-off boat service that operates along the Seine River, with stops at major landmarks and attractions. You can purchase a ticket and board the Batobus at any of its designated stops, such as the Eiffel Tower, Louvre Museum, Notre-Dame Cathedral, and more.

**2. Bateaux Parisiens or Vedettes de Paris:** These are popular cruise operators that offer sightseeing tours along the Seine River, showcasing famous landmarks like the Eiffel Tower, Musée d'Orsay, and Île de la Cité. You can board these boats at their respective docks near key attractions in Paris.

**3. Metro/RER Stations:** Some of the Seine River cruise companies have boarding points near metro or RER (suburban train) stations. For example, the Bateaux Parisiens dock is near the Trocadéro metro station, providing easy access to those arriving by public transport.

As you glide along the Seine River, you'll be treated to breathtaking views of Paris's architectural wonders, including historic bridges, grand palaces, and charming riverside promenades. The cruise offers a leisurely way to see the city's landmarks and soak in the enchanting ambiance of Paris from a different vantage point.

Whether you opt for a narrated tour or a simple sightseeing cruise, a journey along the Seine River promises a memorable experience that captures the romantic essence of Paris. Don't forget to have your camera ready to capture the beauty of the city from the water as you sail past iconic landmarks and under elegant bridges that define the quintessential Parisian charm.

## 5.7 More Hidden Gems

Paris is a city full of hidden gems waiting to be discovered, and you can easily explore these lesser-known treasures via train. Here are a few hidden gems in Paris that you can reach by train:

1. Parc des Buttes-Chaumont: Take the metro Line 7 to the Buttes Chaumont station, located in the 19th arrondissement. This park is a peaceful oasis in the city, featuring a hilly landscape, a picturesque lake with a temple on an island, and stunning views of Paris. Perfect for a leisurely stroll or a picnic away from the crowds.

**2. Cité Universitaire:** Located near the RER B station Cité Universitaire, this complex houses different university residences designed by renowned architects from around the world. Each building represents a different country and architectural style, making it a fascinating place for architecture enthusiasts and those seeking a unique cultural experience away from the typical tourist attractions.

**3. Marché aux Puces de Saint-Ouen (Saint-Ouen Flea Market):** Hop on metro Line 4 to the Porte de Clignancourt station, where you'll find one of the largest and most famous flea markets in Paris. Explore the labyrinthine alleys filled with vintage treasures, antiques, and unique finds that make this market a haven for collectors, bargain hunters, and anyone looking for a one-of-a-kind souvenir.

**4. La Petite Ceinture:** Accessible from various points along its route, La Petite Ceinture is a former railway line that circles Paris and has been transformed into a nature walk and cycling path. You can access different sections of this hidden gem via train stations like Porte de Vanves, Porte de la Villette, or Pereire-Levallois, offering a glimpse into a quieter side of the city with green spaces and urban exploration opportunities.

5. Musée de la Chasse et de la Nature (Museum of Hunting and Nature): Take the metro Line 1 to the Saint-Paul station to visit this unique museum dedicated to the history of hunting and its depiction in art. Housed in a historic mansion in the Marais district, the museum features an eclectic collection of artworks, taxidermy, and objects related to the hunting tradition, providing a fascinating and offbeat cultural experience.

Exploring these hidden gems in Paris via train not only offers you a chance to discover a different side of the city but also allows you to immerse yourself in local culture, history, and artistic expressions that may not be as widely known to visitors. Each of these destinations provides a memorable and authentic experience that showcases the diverse and captivating essence of Paris beyond its well-trodden paths.

# Chapter 6 Day Trips from Paris

## 6.1 Versailles: The Palace and Gardens

A day trip from Paris to Versailles to visit the Palace and its magnificent gardens is a popular and rewarding experience. Here's how to plan your excursion to the Palace of Versailles:

1. Getting There: The easiest way to reach Versailles from Paris is by train. You can take the RER C line from central Paris to Versailles-Rive Gauche station, which is located near the entrance to the palace. The journey takes approximately 45 minutes, making it convenient for a day trip.

2. Visiting the Palace: Upon arrival, make your way to the Palace of Versailles, a UNESCO World Heritage site known for its opulent architecture and historical significance. Explore the State Apartments, Hall of Mirrors, King's and Queen's Grand Apartments, and the Royal Chapel to admire the lavish interiors and learn about the palace's royal history.

3. The Gardens: After touring the palace, don't miss the chance to wander through the expansive Gardens of Versailles. Designed in the classic French style, the gardens feature fountains, sculptures, manicured lawns, and ornamental flower beds spread across acres of lush greenery. You can rent a golf cart or bicycle to explore the vast grounds or simply take a leisurely stroll to enjoy the serene beauty of the landscape.

4. Musical Fountains Show: If you visit Versailles during the summer months, consider planning your trip on a day when the Musical Fountains Show is scheduled. This special event features synchronized music and water displays at various fountains throughout the gardens, adding an enchanting touch to your visit and showcasing the grandeur of Versailles in a unique way.

5. Trianon Palaces and Marie-Antoinette's Estate: For a more comprehensive experience, extend your visit to include the Trianon Palaces and the Estate of Marie-Antoinette. Located within the larger grounds of Versailles, these smaller palaces and gardens offer a glimpse into the private lives of the French royals and provide a different perspective on the estate's history and architectural beauty.

**6. Local Dining:** Before heading back to Paris, take the opportunity to enjoy a meal at one of the charming restaurants or cafes in Versailles. Indulge in traditional French cuisine or opt for a leisurely picnic in the gardens for a memorable dining experience in this historic setting.

Visiting Versailles from Paris allows you to immerse yourself in the grandeur of French history and culture, exploring one of the most iconic royal residences in Europe and experiencing the beauty of its meticulously designed gardens. Whether you're interested in art, architecture, history, or simply seeking a peaceful retreat from the bustle of the city, a day trip to Versailles offers a memorable and enriching excursion that showcases the splendor of France's royal heritage.

## 6.2 Getting to Versailles by Train

Traveling from Paris to Versailles by train is a convenient and popular option for visitors looking to explore the Palace of Versailles and its stunning gardens. Here's a guide on how to easily cruise the train journey from Paris to Versailles:

1. RER C Line: The most common way to reach Versailles from Paris is by taking the RER C train line. The RER C line has several branches, so make sure you board a train that is heading towards Versailles-Rive Gauche station, which is the closest station to the Palace of Versailles.

2. Departure Stations: In Paris, you can catch the RER C train from various stations, including major hubs like Invalides, Musee d'Orsay, or Champ de Mars-Tour Eiffel. You can choose the station that is most convenient for you based on your location in Paris.

3. Travel Time: The journey from Paris to Versailles by train typically takes around 45 minutes, depending on your departure station and any potential delays. Trains run frequently throughout the day, making it easy to plan your visit to Versailles at your preferred time.

4. Tickets: To travel on the RER C line, you can purchase tickets at the train station from ticket machines or staffed counters. Make sure to select a ticket that covers Zone 4, as Versailles is located outside the central Paris zones. You can also use a

Paris Visite pass or Navigo Decouverte card for unlimited travel within the specified zones.

5. Arrival at Versailles-Rive Gauche: Once you arrive at Versailles-Rive Gauche station, follow the signs to the exit and make your way towards the Palace of Versailles. The station is located within walking distance of the palace entrance, so you can easily reach your destination on foot.

6. Return Journey: When you're ready to head back to Paris, simply return to Versailles-Rive Gauche station and board a train heading towards Paris on the RER C line. Trains typically run until late evening, allowing you to enjoy a full day trip to Versailles and return to Paris comfortably.

7. Additional Tips: To make the most of your train journey to Versailles, consider checking the train schedule in advance to plan your day efficiently. Be aware of peak travel times, especially during rush hours, and aim for a more leisurely journey if possible.

Traveling to Versailles by train offers a convenient and budget-friendly way to explore this iconic French destination from Paris. Whether you're interested in history, art, or simply want to enjoy the beauty of the palace and gardens, a day trip to Versailles by train allows you to immerse yourself in the grandeur of French royal history while experiencing the charm of this historic landmark.

## 6.3 Exploring the Palace and Grounds

Once you arrive at the Palace of Versailles, you will be greeted by the sheer opulence and grandeur of this historic landmark, which served as the royal residence of French kings and queens. Here's a guide on how to explore the palace and its sprawling gardens to make the most of your visit:

1. Palace of Versailles: Start your visit by exploring the Palace of Versailles, known for its lavish architecture, ornate decor, and rich history. Highlights of the palace include the Hall of Mirrors, the King's and Queen's Apartments, the Royal Chapel, and the stunning gardens visible from the palace windows.

2. Hall of Mirrors: One of the most iconic rooms in the palace, the Hall of Mirrors is lined with 17 mirrored arches that reflect the palace gardens and the Palace terrace. Admire the intricate ceiling paintings and crystal chandeliers while learning

about the historical events that took place in this grand hall.

3. King's and Queen's Apartments: Explore the opulent living quarters of King Louis XIV and Queen Marie Antoinette, which are filled with period furniture, exquisite tapestries, and elaborate decorations. Gain insight into the luxurious lifestyle of the French royals as you wander through these regal rooms.

4. Royal Chapel: Visit the Royal Chapel, a masterpiece of Baroque architecture, where the royal family attended religious ceremonies and masses. Admire the intricate carvings, sculptures, and stained glass windows that adorn this sacred space.

5. Gardens and Park: After touring the palace, venture out into the expansive gardens and park of Versailles, designed in the classic French formal style. Explore the meticulously manicured lawns, fountains, sculptures, and flower beds that adorn the outdoor spaces surrounding the palace.

6. Grand Trianon and Petit Trianon: For a more intimate look at royal life, visit the Grand Trianon and Petit Trianon, two smaller palaces located within the Versailles grounds. These retreats were used by

the French monarchs for private gatherings and leisure activities away from the main palace.

7. Musical Fountains Show: If you're visiting Versailles during the summer months, consider attending the Musical Fountains Show, a spectacular display of music, water, and light in the palace gardens. This special event brings the historic fountains to life in a magical performance that transports visitors back to the time of the French monarchy.

8. Eating and Shopping: Take a break from sightseeing and enjoy a meal at the palace's on-site restaurants and cafes, offering a selection of French cuisine and refreshments. You can also browse the gift shops for souvenirs, books, and royal-themed merchandise to commemorate your visit to Versailles.

Exploring the Palace of Versailles and its grounds is a captivating journey through French history, art, and culture, providing a glimpse into the extravagant world of the French monarchy. Whether you're interested in architecture, history, or simply enjoy the beauty of majestic palaces and gardens, a visit to Versailles offers a truly unforgettable experience that will leave you in awe of its grandeur and beauty.

## 6.4 Disneyland Paris: A Magical Day Out

Commence on a magical journey to Disneyland Paris, where fairy tales come to life and dreams come true. Here's how to make the most of your day at this enchanting theme park:

1. Main Street, U.S.A.: Begin your day by strolling down Main Street, U.S.A., a charming thoroughfare lined with shops, restaurants, and entertainment. Take in the nostalgic Americana atmosphere and snap a photo in front of Sleeping Beauty Castle, the iconic centerpiece of Disneyland Paris.

2. Attractions: Disneyland Paris offers a wide range of attractions for all ages, from thrilling roller coasters to classic dark rides. Be sure to check out popular rides like Space Mountain: Mission 2, Big Thunder Mountain, Pirates of the Caribbean, and It's a Small World. FastPasses are available for select attractions to help you maximize your time in the park.

3. Shows and Parades: Don't miss the spectacular shows and parades that take place throughout the day at Disneyland Paris. Catch the dazzling Disney Illuminations nighttime show, featuring fireworks, projections, and special effects set to beloved Disney

music. Be sure to check the schedule for other entertainment offerings, such as character meet-and-greets and stage performances.

4. Fantasyland: Immerse yourself in the magical world of Fantasyland, where fairy tales come to life. Explore attractions like Peter Pan's Flight, Dumbo the Flying Elephant, and Sleeping Beauty Castle, and don't forget to meet your favorite Disney princesses at Auberge de Cendrillon.

5. Adventureland: kickstart on exciting adventures in Adventureland, where you can explore exotic jungles, encounter pirates, and brave thrilling rides. Ride the Pirates of the Caribbean attraction, explore the Swiss Family Treehouse, and set sail on the Adventure Isle river raft adventure.

6. Discoveryland: Step into the future in Discoveryland, a futuristic land inspired by the works of Jules Verne and Leonardo da Vinci. Ride the iconic Space Mountain: Mission 2 roller coaster, soar above the park on Orbitron, and pilot your own spaceship on Buzz Lightyear Laser Blast.

7. Dining: Fuel your magical day with delicious dining options throughout the park, including themed restaurants, quick-service eateries, and snack

carts. Indulge in classic Disney treats like Mickey-shaped waffles, churros, and popcorn, or enjoy a sit-down meal at one of the park's themed restaurants.

8. Shopping: Take home a piece of the magic by exploring the shops and boutiques at Disneyland Paris. Browse for souvenirs, apparel, toys, and accessories featuring your favorite Disney characters and attractions. Don't forget to pick up exclusive merchandise only available at Disneyland Paris.

9. Photo Opportunities: Capture memories of your day at Disneyland Paris by posing for photos with Disney characters, in front of iconic landmarks, and during special meet-and-greet experiences. PhotoPass photographers are stationed throughout the park to help you capture the magic of your visit.

10. Fireworks Display: End your magical day at Disneyland Paris with a spectacular fireworks display that lights up the night sky above Sleeping Beauty Castle. Watch in awe as the sky is filled with colorful bursts of light, music, and magic, creating a truly unforgettable finale to your Disney adventure.

A visit to Disneyland Paris promises a day filled with joy, wonder, and enchantment, where guests of all ages can experience the magic of Disney come to life.

Whether you're a thrill-seeker, a fan of classic Disney characters, or simply looking to immerse yourself in a world of fantasy and fun, Disneyland Paris offers something special for everyone to enjoy.

## 6.5 Trains to Disneyland

Traveling to Disneyland Paris by train is a convenient and scenic way to reach the magical theme park. Here is all you need to know about taking the train to Disneyland Paris:

1. Eurostar: If you are traveling from London or other cities in the United Kingdom, the Eurostar high-speed train service offers direct connections to Disneyland Paris. The Eurostar service runs from London St Pancras International to Marne-la-Vallée Chessy station, located just a short walk from the entrance to Disneyland Paris. The journey takes approximately 2 hours and offers a comfortable and efficient way to travel to the park.

2. TGV: If you are traveling from within France or other European cities, you can take a TGV (Train à Grande Vitesse) high-speed train to Marne-la-Vallée Chessy station. The TGV service provides fast and convenient connections to Disneyland Paris from

major cities such as Paris, Lyon, Marseille, and Brussels. The station is located conveniently close to the theme park, making it easy to access upon arrival.

3. RER: The RER (Réseau Express Régional) regional train service also connects Paris to Disneyland Paris. You can take the RER A line from central Paris to Marne-la-Vallée Chessy station, which is the final stop on the line. The journey takes approximately 40-45 minutes and offers an affordable way to reach the theme park from the city center.

4. Tickets: Tickets for train travel to Disneyland Paris can be purchased in advance online or at the train station. It is recommended to book your tickets early, especially during peak travel times, to secure the best prices and availability. Consider purchasing special Disney-themed train tickets for an added touch of magic to your journey.

5. Schedules: Trains to Disneyland Paris operate throughout the day, with frequent departures from major cities and stations. Be sure to check the train schedules in advance to plan your journey and coordinate your arrival with the park's opening hours. You can easily access train schedules, routes,

and ticket information on the official train operator websites or through travel planning apps.

6. Luggage: When traveling to Disneyland Paris by train, be mindful of luggage restrictions and storage options on board the trains. Most trains offer ample space for luggage, including overhead racks and dedicated storage areas. However, it is advisable to pack light and only bring essential items to ensure a comfortable and hassle-free journey.

7. Accessibility: The train stations at Disneyland Paris are equipped with facilities to accommodate passengers with mobility needs and disabilities. Accessible restrooms, elevators, and ramps are available at the stations to ensure a smooth experience for all travelers. If you require special assistance or accommodations, be sure to notify the train operator in advance to make necessary arrangements.

8. Additional Tips: Remember to validate your train ticket before boarding the train, especially if you are using paper tickets or contactless cards. Keep your ticket handy for inspection during the journey, and follow any instructions or guidelines provided by the train staff. Enjoy the scenic views along the way and

get ready to immerse yourself in the magic of Disneyland Paris upon arrival.

Traveling to Disneyland Paris by train offers a convenient, comfortable, and enjoyable way to reach the beloved theme park. Whether you are coming from within France, the United Kingdom, or other European cities, the train provides a stress-free alternative to driving and allows you to relax and enjoy the journey as you anticipate the magical experiences awaiting you at Disneyland Paris.

## 6.6 Tips for Enjoying Disneyland Paris by Rail

Here are some tips to help you make the most of your Disneyland Paris experience when traveling by rail:

**1. Plan Your Journey:** Before setting off, familiarize yourself with the train schedules and connections to ensure a smooth and timely journey to Disneyland Paris. Check for any updates or disruptions that may affect your travel plans and allow ample time to reach the park.

**2. Pack Essentials:** When traveling to Disneyland Paris by train, pack essentials such as your tickets,

ID, phone, charger, comfortable clothing and shoes, snacks, and any necessary medication. Consider bringing a refillable water bottle to stay hydrated throughout the day.

3. Check Park Hours: Verify the park's operating hours and schedule any must-see attractions, shows, or parades you don't want to miss. Arrive early to take advantage of shorter queues and make the most of your visit.

4. Use FastPass: Disneyland Paris offers a FastPass system that allows you to skip the regular queue for select attractions by reserving a time slot. Make use of FastPass to minimize wait times and maximize your time enjoying the rides and attractions.

5. Download the Disneyland Paris App: Download the official Disneyland Paris app to access park maps, attraction wait times, show schedules, dining options, and real-time updates during your visit. The app can help you plan your day efficiently and cruise the park with ease.

6. Stay Flexible: While it's great to have a plan, be prepared to adjust it based on ride wait times, show schedules, and unexpected surprises. Stay flexible

and adapt to make the most of your time at Disneyland Paris.

7. **Explore Both Parks:** Disneyland Paris consists of two theme parks, Disneyland Park and Walt Disney Studios Park. Be sure to explore both parks to enjoy a variety of attractions, shows, and experiences tailored to different themes and interests.

8. **Take Breaks:** With so much to see and do, it's important to take breaks and recharge throughout the day. Find quiet spots to relax, enjoy a snack, or watch a parade to rejuvenate and keep your energy levels up.

9. **Meet Characters:** One of the highlights of visiting Disneyland Paris is meeting beloved Disney characters. Check the character meet-and-greet locations and schedules to have the chance to interact, take photos, and create magical memories with your favorite characters.

10. **Enjoy Dining Options:** Disneyland Paris offers a wide range of dining options, from quick-service snacks to themed restaurants. Explore different dining experiences within the parks and Disney Village to savor delicious meals and treats during your visit.

11. **Stay Hydrated and Sun-Protected:** Keep hydrated by drinking water throughout the day, especially during warmer weather. Apply sunscreen, wear a hat, and seek shade when needed to protect yourself from the sun's rays while enjoying the outdoor attractions.

12. **Plan for Souvenirs:** If you plan to purchase souvenirs or gifts, consider browsing the shops earlier in the day to avoid carrying them around all day. Disneyland Paris offers a variety of themed merchandise, apparel, and keepsakes to commemorate your visit.

13. **Capture Memories:** Don't forget to capture your magical moments at Disneyland Paris through photos and videos. Whether using a camera or smartphone, documenting your experiences allows you to relive the fun and share memories with others.

By following these tips and planning ahead, you can make the most of your Disneyland Paris visit when traveling by train. Enjoy the enchanting atmosphere, thrilling attractions, captivating shows, and memorable encounters with beloved Disney characters for a truly magical experience at the happiest place on earth.

## 6.7 Giverny: Monet's Garden

Giverny, located in the picturesque region of Normandy, France, is famously known as the home of renowned Impressionist artist Claude Monet. Visitors flock to Giverny to immerse themselves in Monet's world and explore the stunning gardens that inspired some of his most iconic works. Here are some tips for enjoying a visit to Monet's Garden in Giverny:

**1. Plan Your Visit:** Before heading to Giverny, check the opening hours and seasonal availability of Monet's Garden. It is advisable to visit during the spring and summer months when the gardens are in full bloom, showcasing a kaleidoscope of colors and fragrances.

**2. Tickets and Reservations:** Purchase your tickets in advance to avoid long queues, especially during peak tourist seasons. Consider booking a guided tour to gain insights into Monet's life, art, and the significance of his gardens.

**3. Getting There:** Giverny is easily accessible by train from Paris, with a journey lasting approximately one to two hours. Alternatively, you can opt for a guided tour or rent a car for a more flexible travel experience.

4. **Exploring the Gardens:** Take your time wandering through the Clos Normand flower garden, featuring a symphony of flowers arranged in vibrant color schemes. Meander along the Japanese-inspired water garden, with its iconic water lilies, Japanese bridge, and serene pond that inspired Monet's famous paintings.

5. **Photography Tips:** Capture the beauty of Monet's Garden by bringing a camera or smartphone to take photos of the blooming flowers, meandering pathways, reflective ponds, and charming details that epitomize the essence of Impressionist art. Early morning or late afternoon light can enhance the magical atmosphere of the gardens.

6. **Respect the Environment:** While exploring Monet's Garden, be mindful of the surroundings and follow the designated pathways to preserve the delicate flora and fauna. Avoid picking flowers or disturbing the natural setting to maintain the integrity of the garden for future visitors.

7. **Visit the House:** Explore Monet's former residence, a charming pink house filled with period furnishings,

personal belongings, and artwork that provide a glimpse into the artist's daily life and creative process. Don't miss the opportunity to view Monet's studio, where he painted many of his masterpieces.

8. Gift Shop and Cafés: Browse the gift shop for souvenirs, books, and Monet-inspired merchandise to commemorate your visit to Giverny. Relax and enjoy a meal or refreshments at one of the on-site cafés overlooking the gardens for a delightful break during your exploration.

9. Additional Attractions: Extend your visit to Giverny by exploring the surrounding area, including the Museum of Impressionisms Giverny, showcasing works by Impressionist artists, and the charming village with its quaint shops, galleries, and cafes.

10. Weather Considerations: Be prepared for changing weather conditions in Normandy, including rain showers or cooler temperatures, especially during the shoulder seasons. Bring appropriate clothing, an umbrella, and sunscreen to ensure a comfortable and enjoyable visit.

11. Guided Tours and Workshops: Consider participating in guided tours, workshops, or art classes offered in Giverny to deepen your

understanding of Monet's artistic techniques, gardening principles, and the significance of Impressionism in art history.

12. Reflect and Relax: Take moments to sit, reflect, and absorb the tranquility and beauty of Monet's Garden. Find a peaceful spot to unwind, sketch, or simply savor the sensory delights of nature that inspired Monet's artistic vision and continue to enchant visitors from around the world.

Visiting Monet's Garden in Giverny is an immersive experience that offers a glimpse into the artistic legacy of Claude Monet and the natural beauty that inspired his iconic paintings. Embrace the enchanting atmosphere, vibrant colors, and serene landscapes that continue to captivate visitors seeking inspiration and tranquility in this idyllic corner of France.

## 6.8 Visiting Giverny by Rail

Traveling to Giverny by rail is a convenient and scenic way to reach this charming destination and explore Monet's Garden. Here are some tips for making the most of your visit to Giverny by rail:

1. Train Options: From Paris, you can take a train to Vernon, the nearest train station to Giverny. Trains to Vernon depart from Gare Saint-Lazare station in Paris, and the journey typically takes around 50 minutes to 1.5 hours, depending on the train type.

2. Train Schedule: Check the train schedule in advance to plan your journey to align with the opening hours of Monet's Garden. Trains to Vernon run regularly throughout the day, with more frequent services during peak travel times.

3. Tickets: Purchase your train tickets to Vernon in advance to secure your seat and potentially benefit from discounted fares. You can buy tickets at the train station, online, or through mobile apps for added convenience.

4. Connections: Depending on your starting point in Paris, you may need to transfer trains at a major station like Mantes-la-Jolie or Rouen. Ensure you have ample time between connections to avoid rushing and missing your train to Vernon.

5. Comfort: Choose a comfortable seat on the train to relax and enjoy the scenic journey through the French countryside. Opt for a window seat to admire

the rolling hills, quaint villages, and picturesque landscapes along the way.

6. Pack Essentials: Bring essentials for your day trip to Giverny, including a camera, water bottle, snacks, comfortable walking shoes, sunscreen, and a light jacket or umbrella in case of changing weather conditions.

7. Vernon Station: Upon arriving at Vernon station, follow signs to the bus stop outside the station, where you can catch a shuttle bus to Giverny. The bus ride to Giverny takes approximately 15-20 minutes and drops you off near the entrance to Monet's Garden.

8. Bus Schedule: Be mindful of the bus schedule between Vernon station and Giverny, as buses may have limited frequency, especially on weekends and public holidays. Plan your return journey accordingly to catch the bus back to Vernon station.

9. Entry Tickets: Purchase your entry tickets to Monet's Garden online in advance or at the ticket office upon arrival. Consider opting for a combined ticket that includes access to both the Clos Normand flower garden and the water garden to fully immerse yourself in Monet's world.

**10. Guided Tours:** If you prefer a guided experience, join a guided tour of Monet's Garden offered by local tour operators or book a tour package that includes transportation, entry tickets, and a guided visit of the gardens and Monet's house.

**11. Explore Giverny:** After visiting Monet's Garden, take time to explore the charming village of Giverny, with its boutiques, art galleries, cafes, and the Museum of Impressionisms Giverny to probe deeper into the world of Impressionist art.

**12. Return Journey:** Plan your return journey from Giverny to Vernon station to catch your train back to Paris. Check the train schedule for return trips and factor in travel time from Giverny to Vernon to ensure a stress-free journey back.

Traveling to Giverny by rail offers a hassle-free and enjoyable way to experience Monet's Garden and immerse yourself in the beauty and inspiration that captivated Claude Monet. Embrace the tranquility of the gardens, appreciate the vibrant colors of the flowers, and savor the artistic legacy that continues to enchant visitors from around the world.

## 6.9 Exploring Monet's Home and Gardens

Exploring Monet's home and gardens in Giverny is a delightful experience that offers a glimpse into the world that inspired the renowned Impressionist painter. Here are some tips to make the most of your visit:

1. Monet's House: Start your visit by exploring Monet's pink-hued house, where the artist lived with his family for over 40 years. Wander through the rooms filled with original furniture, family photos, and Japanese prints that Monet collected.

2. Kitchen: Don't miss the charming blue-tiled kitchen, where you can see the old stove, copper pots, and colorful ceramic dishes that evoke a sense of warmth and domestic life in the late 19th and early 20th centuries.

3. Monet's Studios: Explore the two studios where Monet created his masterpieces, filled with natural light and overlooking the gardens. Imagine the artist at work as you admire the easels, paintbrushes, and unfinished paintings that offer a glimpse into his creative process.

4. Clos Normand: Step outside to the Clos Normand, Monet's flower garden bursting with a riot of colors and textures. Marvel at the meticulously planned flower beds, including tulips, roses, poppies, and irises, arranged in harmonious palettes that inspired many of his paintings.

5. Water Garden: Cross the iconic Japanese bridge to reach Monet's iconic water garden, where you'll encounter weeping willows, water lilies, and serene ponds that provided the artist with endless inspiration for his famous "Water Lilies" series.

6. Pond with Water Lilies: Sit by the tranquil pond where Monet painted his water lily canvases, capturing the play of light, reflections, and changing seasons that became hallmarks of his Impressionist style. Take a moment to absorb the peaceful ambiance and natural beauty that influenced his artistic vision.

7. Claude Monet's Inspiration: Reflect on the sights and sounds that inspired Monet as you stroll through the gardens, listening to birdsong, feeling the gentle breeze, and observing the interplay of colors and textures that he so masterfully translated onto canvas.

8. Photography: Capture the beauty of Monet's gardens with your camera, but also take time to put down your device and simply absorb the essence of the place. Embrace the sensory experience of being surrounded by nature, art, and history.

9. Seasonal Changes: Visit Monet's home and gardens at different times of the year to witness the seasonal changes in flora and fauna, from the vibrant blooms of spring to the golden hues of autumn. Each season offers a unique perspective on Monet's beloved sanctuary.

10. Artistic Inspiration: Allow yourself to be inspired by Monet's artistic legacy as you wander through the gardens and imagine the process of translating nature's beauty onto canvas. Find moments of stillness and contemplation to connect with your own creativity and appreciation for art.

Exploring Monet's home and gardens in Giverny is a soul-stirring experience that invites you to step into the world of a visionary artist and immerse yourself in the beauty that captured his imagination. Take your time to relish the gardens, absorb the ambiance, and savor the artistic essence that continues to enchant visitors from far and wide.

# Chapter 7 Experiencing Parisian Culture

## 7.1 Parisian Cuisine: Foodie's Guide by Rail

Experiencing Parisian culture through its culinary delights is an unforgettable journey that tantalizes the taste buds and showcases the city's rich gastronomic heritage. Here's a foodie's guide to exploring Parisian cuisine by rail:

1. Arrival in Paris: As you arrive in Paris by rail, let the sights, sounds, and smells of the city awaken your appetite for culinary adventures. Begin your gastronomic exploration by heading to a local café or boulangerie for a classic French breakfast of croissants, café au lait, and freshly squeezed orange juice.

2. Markets and Bistros: Start on a culinary tour of Paris's vibrant markets, such as Marché d'Aligre or Marché des Enfants Rouges, where you can sample artisanal cheeses, charcuterie, and fresh produce. After exploring the markets, savor a traditional French lunch at a cozy bistro, where you can indulge

in dishes like boeuf bourguignon, coq au vin, or steak frites.

3. Wine Tasting: Take a break from your culinary exploration to indulge in a wine tasting experience at one of Paris's wine bars or cellars. Discover the diverse flavors of French wines, from Bordeaux to Burgundy, and learn about the art of wine pairing with local cheeses and charcuterie.

4. Cooking Class: Immerse yourself in the art of French cooking by taking a hands-on cooking class in Paris. Learn to prepare classic dishes like ratatouille, quiche Lorraine, or tarte Tatin under the guidance of a skilled chef, and savor the fruits of your labor during a convivial meal with fellow food enthusiasts.

5. Patisseries and Macarons: Indulge your sweet tooth with a visit to Paris's renowned patisseries, where you can sample decadent pastries, cakes, and macarons in a rainbow of flavors and colors. Treat yourself to a box of delicate macarons from Laduree or Pierre Hermé to enjoy as a delicious souvenir of your culinary journey.

6. Cheese and Chocolate Tasting: Probe into the world of French cheese and chocolate by attending a tasting session at a specialty fromagerie or

chocolaterie. Sample a variety of cheeses, from creamy brie to tangy Roquefort, paired with artisanal chocolates infused with flavors like lavender, sea salt, or exotic spices.

7. Cocktail Bars and Speakeasies: Experience Paris's thriving cocktail culture by visiting one of the city's chic cocktail bars or hidden speakeasies. Sip on expertly crafted cocktails made with premium spirits, fresh herbs, and house-made syrups while soaking up the sophisticated ambiance of Paris by night.

8. Street Food and Food Trucks: Explore Paris's vibrant street food scene by seeking out food trucks and market stalls serving up gourmet treats from around the world. Indulge in Vietnamese banh mi, Moroccan couscous, or Lebanese falafel as you roam the city's bustling streets and squares.

9. Dining on the Seine: Treat yourself to a memorable dining experience aboard a Seine River cruise, where you can savor a gourmet meal while taking in panoramic views of Paris's iconic landmarks. Enjoy French cuisine at its finest as you glide past Notre Dame, the Eiffel Tower, and the Louvre under the starry Parisian sky.

10. Food Markets by Rail: Extend your culinary adventure beyond Paris by taking a day trip to one of the charming food markets in the surrounding regions, such as Versailles, Saint-Germain-en-Laye, or Rambouillet. Explore the stalls brimming with local delicacies, from artisanal cheeses and rustic bread to seasonal fruits and vegetables, and savor the authentic flavors of the French countryside.

Indulging in Parisian cuisine by rail is a gourmet's dream come true, offering a feast for the senses that celebrates the artistry, tradition, and creativity of French gastronomy. So hop on the train, commence on a culinary journey through the heart of Paris, and savor every delectable moment along the way. Bon appétit!

## 7.2 French Culinary Delights to Try

French cuisine is celebrated worldwide for its sophistication, creativity, and exquisite flavors. Here are some French culinary delights you must try to experience the essence of this rich gastronomic tradition:

1. Croissant: A quintessential French pastry, the buttery and flaky croissant is a must-try delicacy that

is perfect for breakfast or a snack. Pair it with a café au lait for an authentic French experience.

2. Escargot: If you're feeling adventurous, try escargot, cooked land snails typically served with garlic butter and parsley. This classic French dish is a delicacy known for its unique texture and flavor.

3. Coq au Vin: A hearty and flavorful dish, coq au vin is a traditional French stew made with chicken, red wine, mushrooms, onions, and bacon. It's a comforting meal that showcases the depth of French culinary techniques.

4. Ratatouille: This colorful and fragrant vegetable stew is a staple of Provençal cuisine. Made with eggplant, zucchini, bell peppers, tomatoes, and aromatic herbs, ratatouille is a light and healthy dish that celebrates the abundance of fresh produce.

5. Foie Gras: A luxurious delicacy made from the fattened liver of a duck or goose, foie gras is a refined and indulgent treat often served as a pâté or terrine. Its rich and buttery flavor is a true embodiment of French haute cuisine.

6. Bouillabaisse: A seafood lover's delight, bouillabaisse is a traditional Provençal fish stew

made with a variety of fish and shellfish, flavored with saffron, garlic, and herbs. Enjoy this aromatic dish with a side of rouille, a spicy garlic mayonnaise.

7. Cassoulet: Hearty and rustic, cassoulet is a flavorful stew of white beans, duck confit, sausage, and pork, slow-cooked to tender perfection. This traditional dish from the southwest of France is a comforting and satisfying meal.

8. Tarte Tatin: A classic French dessert, tarte Tatin is an upside-down caramelized apple tart that is buttery, sweet, and decadent. Served warm with a dollop of crème fraîche or vanilla ice cream, it's a delightful finale to any meal.

9. Crème Brûlée: Indulge in the luscious and creamy goodness of crème brûlée, a silky smooth custard topped with a layer of caramelized sugar. Break through the crackling sugar crust to reveal the velvety custard beneath for a truly luxurious dessert experience.

10. Macarons: Delicate and colorful macarons are a beloved French treat made from almond meringue shells sandwiched together with ganache, buttercream, or jam. These dainty confections come in a variety of flavors, from classic pistachio and

raspberry to inventive creations like salted caramel and rose lychee.

Whether you're savoring a buttery croissant for breakfast, indulging in a decadent slice of tarte Tatin for dessert, or enjoying a comforting bowl of coq au vin for dinner, exploring French culinary delights is a journey of sensory delights and gastronomic pleasures. Bon appétit!

## 7.3 Best Restaurants and Cafés Accessible by Rail

Paris is a culinary paradise with a plethora of exquisite restaurants and charming cafes that can be easily accessed by the city's comprehensive rail network. Here are some top recommendations for dining establishments in Paris that are conveniently located near train stations:

1. Le Train Bleu:
- Location: Gare de Lyon Train Station
- Description: Step back in time and dine in opulent surroundings at Le Train Bleu, a historic restaurant known for its stunning Belle Époque decor and classic French cuisine. Indulge in dishes like foie gras,

escargots, and beef tournedos while enjoying the grand ambiance of this iconic Parisian establishment.

2. Angelina:
- Location: Near the Louvre Museum
- Description: For a delightful tea and pastry experience, head to Angelina, a renowned tearoom near the Louvre. Treat yourself to their famous hot chocolate "L'Africain" and decadent pastries like the Mont-Blanc while basking in the elegant Belle Époque setting.

3. Terminus Nord:
- Location: Gare du Nord Train Station
- Description: Located right at Gare du Nord, Terminus Nord is a bustling brasserie that exudes Parisian charm. Enjoy classic brasserie fare like steak frites, onion soup, and fresh seafood in a vibrant setting that captures the essence of traditional French dining.

4. Le Grand Colbert:
- Location: Châtelet-Les Halles Train Station
- Description: Situated near the bustling Châtelet-Les Halles station, Le Grand Colbert is a beloved Parisian institution known for its elegant Belle Époque decor and delicious French cuisine. Savour

classic dishes such as steak tartare, duck confit, and profiteroles in this timeless setting.

5. La Gare:
- Location: Near Invalides Train Station
- Description: La Gare is a chic restaurant housed in a former railway station near Invalides. Enjoy modern French cuisine in a stylish setting that pays homage to its historical roots. Indulge in dishes like pan-seared sea bass, roasted rack of lamb, and decadent desserts while soaking in the unique atmosphere.

6. Café de la Paix:
- Location: Opéra Garnier
- Description: Adjacent to the iconic Opéra Garnier, Café de la Paix is a Parisian institution known for its elegant setting and delectable French cuisine. Enjoy a leisurely meal of classic dishes like beef bourguignon, foie gras terrine, and tarte Tatin amidst the grandeur of this historic establishment.

7. Le Bouillon Chartier:
- Location: Near Grands Boulevards Train Station
- Description: Experience a taste of old Paris at Le Bouillon Chartier, a legendary brasserie near Grands Boulevards station. Feast on affordable French classics like escargots, coq au vin, and crème brûlée

in a bustling, art deco setting that has charmed diners for over a century.

Indulge in the diverse culinary offerings of Paris by exploring these exceptional restaurants and cafes that are easily accessible by rail. Whether you're in the mood for haute cuisine in a historic setting or a relaxed meal in a bustling brasserie, these dining destinations capture the essence of French gastronomy amidst the vibrant backdrop of the City of Light. Bon appétit!

## 7.4 Shopping in Paris: Chic Boutiques and Markets

Paris is a fashion mecca renowned for its chic boutiques, stylish department stores, and bustling markets that cater to every taste and budget. Whether you're looking for high-end designer labels, unique vintage finds, or trendy streetwear, the city offers a wealth of shopping options that can be easily accessed by its efficient public transport system. Here are some must-visit destinations for shopping in Paris:

1. Le Marais:

- Description: This historic district is a treasure trove of trendy boutiques, vintage stores, and artisan shops. Explore the winding cobblestone streets to discover a mix of established designers and emerging labels, as well as art galleries and concept stores. Le Marais is a hub of creativity and style, perfect for fashion-forward shoppers.

2. Galeries Lafayette:
- Location: Boulevard Haussmann
- Description: A Parisian institution, Galeries Lafayette is a luxury department store that offers a premium shopping experience under its iconic glass dome. Browse through a curated selection of designer fashion, accessories, beauty products, and gourmet treats in a grand setting that epitomizes Parisian elegance.

3. Saint-Ouen Flea Market (Les Puces de Saint-Ouen):
- Location: Porte de Clignancourt
- Description: For vintage lovers and treasure hunters, the Saint-Ouen Flea Market is a paradise of antiques, vintage clothing, and unique collectibles. Explore the maze of stalls to unearth one-of-a-kind finds and timeless pieces that reflect Paris's rich cultural heritage.

**4. Rue du Faubourg Saint-Honoré:**
- Description: This prestigious shopping street is home to luxury fashion houses, exclusive boutiques, and renowned designer flagship stores. Stroll along Rue du Faubourg Saint-Honoré to admire the latest collections from haute couture brands and indulge in a luxury shopping experience that epitomizes Parisian elegance.

**5. Le Bon Marché:**
- Location: Rue de Sèvres
- Description: The oldest department store in Paris, Le Bon Marché is a haven for luxury shopping and unique finds. Explore the curated selection of fashion, beauty, home decor, and gourmet delicacies in a sophisticated setting that showcases the best of French and international design.

**6. Marché aux Puces de Montreuil:**
- Location: Porte de Montreuil
- Description: This eclectic flea market offers a diverse range of goods, from vintage clothing and accessories to furniture and artwork. Bargain hunters will delight in the array of stalls selling unique items at affordable prices, making it a hidden gem for those seeking a unique shopping experience.

**7. Avenue des Champs-Élysées:**

- Description: This iconic boulevard is lined with luxury boutiques, flagship stores, and upscale retailers that cater to fashion enthusiasts and trendsetters. Explore the glamorous shopping avenue to discover the latest fashion trends, designer collections, and stylish accessories in a vibrant and cosmopolitan setting.

Immerse yourself in the world of fashion and style in Paris by exploring these diverse shopping destinations that capture the essence of the city's sartorial spirit. Whether you're seeking high-end designer pieces, vintage treasures, or unique artisanal creations, Paris offers a shopping experience like no other. Enjoy the thrill of discovering new fashion finds and coveted keepsakes in the fashion capital of the world. Happy shopping!

## 7.5 Retail Therapy by Rail

Kickstart on a retail therapy adventure by rail in Paris, the epitome of style and fashion. Known for its iconic shopping districts, luxury boutiques, and chic concept stores, Paris offers a shopping experience like no other. Traveling by train within the city provides a convenient and efficient way to explore the diverse shopping scenes while enjoying the charm of the

French capital. Here is a guide to indulging in retail therapy by rail in Paris:

1. Champs-Élysées:
- Description: Begin your shopping journey at the world-famous Champs-Élysées, a tree-lined avenue stretching from the Place de la Concorde to the Arc de Triomphe. Hop on the Paris Métro or RER train to reach this iconic shopping street, lined with luxury boutiques, designer stores, flagship outlets, and trendy cafes. Explore renowned brands like Louis Vuitton, Chanel, and Zara, and savor the Parisian ambiance as you shop along this glamorous boulevard.

2. Le Marais:
- Description: Take a leisurely walk or a short train ride to the historic neighborhood of Le Marais, known for its eclectic mix of designer boutiques, vintage stores, art galleries, and concept stores. Board the Paris Metro or RER to stations like Saint-Paul or Hôtel de Ville to access this trendy district. Discover unique fashion finds, handmade jewelry, contemporary art pieces, and stylish accessories while soaking in the bohemian ambiance of Le Marais.

3. Galeries Lafayette:

- Description: Treat yourself to a shopping spree at Galeries Lafayette, one of Paris's most iconic department stores located near the Opéra Garnier. Easily accessible by the Paris Métro or RER, this luxury shopping destination offers a wide range of fashion brands, beauty products, accessories, home decor, and gourmet food options under one roof. Shop for designer labels, attend fashion events, enjoy panoramic views from the rooftop terrace, and experience the essence of Parisian shopping at Galeries Lafayette.

4. Saint-Germain-des-Prés:
- Description: Explore the artistic and intellectual neighborhood of Saint-Germain-des-Prés, accessible by train to the Saint-Germain-des-Prés or Odéon stations. Wander through charming cobblestone streets lined with upscale boutiques, antique shops, bookstores, and designer ateliers. Discover timeless fashion pieces, artisanal craftsmanship, elegant homeware, and literary treasures in this historic district synonymous with Parisian elegance and sophistication.

5. La Vallée Village:
- Description: Escape the city bustle for a day of outlet shopping at La Vallée Village, located just outside Paris and easily accessible by RER train from

central stations like Gare de Lyon or Châtelet. Indulge in discounted luxury brands, fashion bargains, and exclusive deals at this designer outlet village set in a picturesque open-air setting. Shop for clothing, accessories, shoes, and more from renowned fashion houses while enjoying a relaxing shopping experience away from the city center.

Maneuver the vibrant shopping scenes of Paris by rail and immerse yourself in the exquisite fashion, unique finds, and timeless style that the city has to offer. Whether you're seeking haute couture, trendy streetwear, vintage treasures, or artisanal creations, Paris provides a shopping paradise that caters to every taste and preference. Embrace the elegance and flair of Parisian fashion as you indulge in a memorable retail therapy experience by rail in the City of Light. Happy shopping and bon voyage!

## 7.6 Unique Souvenirs to Bring Home

When traveling to Paris, it's always special to bring home unique souvenirs that capture the essence of the city's culture, art, and lifestyle. From artisanal creations to gourmet delights, here are some ideas for unique souvenirs to consider when visiting the City of Light:

1. Macarons from Ladurée:
- Treat yourself and your loved ones to the delicate and colorful macarons from Ladurée, a renowned French patisserie known for its exquisite pastries. Choose from a variety of flavors packed in beautifully designed boxes as a sweet and iconic souvenir from Paris.

2. Perfume from Fragonard:
- Visit the Fragonard Perfume Museum and boutique to discover the art of French perfumery and bring home a signature scent created in Grasse, the perfume capital of the world. Select a unique fragrance that captures the essence of your Parisian experience.

3. Art Prints from Montmartre:
- Explore the artistic neighborhood of Montmartre and support local artists by purchasing original art prints, watercolors, or sketches depicting iconic Parisian landmarks like the Sacré-Cœur or charming Parisian street scenes. These art pieces make for meaningful and distinctive souvenirs to adorn your walls.

4. French Linens from Le Bon Marché:

- Visit the historic department store Le Bon Marché and shop for luxurious French linens, including tablecloths, napkins, and tea towels that showcase exquisite craftsmanship and timeless elegance. Add a touch of French sophistication to your home with these quality textiles.

5. Vintage Chanel from Les Puces de Saint-Ouen:
- Explore the vast antique market of Les Puces de Saint-Ouen and hunt for vintage fashion treasures, including iconic Chanel pieces like jewelry, handbags, or accessories. Score a unique and timeless fashion souvenir with a touch of Parisian glamour.

6. French Cheese Board Set:
- Discover a gourmet cheese board set featuring a selection of authentic French cheeses such as Brie, Camembert, or Roquefort, paired with artisanal crackers, preserves, and honey. Share the flavors of France with friends and family back home for a delicious and memorable treat.

7. Handcrafted Jewelry from Place Vendôme:
- Explore the luxury jewelry stores around Place Vendôme and invest in a piece of handcrafted jewelry from renowned French designers. Choose from elegant earrings, bracelets, or necklaces that reflect

Parisian style and craftsmanship for a timeless and sophisticated keepsake.

8. Vintage Postcards from Shakespeare and Company:
- Visit the iconic English-language bookstore Shakespeare and Company and browse through its collection of vintage postcards featuring classic Parisian landmarks and literary themes. Send a piece of Parisian charm to your friends or keep them as nostalgic mementos of your trip.

9. French Candles from Diptyque:
- Bring home a luxurious scented candle from Diptyque, a prestigious French fragrance house known for its exquisite candles and home fragrances. Select from a range of captivating scents inspired by nature, travel, and art to infuse your home with a touch of Parisian ambiance.

10. Parisian Fashion Magazine:
- Purchase a copy of a French fashion magazine like Vogue Paris or L'Officiel to stay updated on the latest trends, designers, and style inspirations from the fashion capital of the world. Enjoy flipping through the pages of haute couture and ready-to-wear collections as a chic and informative souvenir.

Each of these unique souvenirs captures a different aspect of Parisian culture, artistry, and lifestyle, allowing you to bring home a piece of the city's charm and elegance. Whether it's a delicious treat, a stylish accessory, or a fragrant memento, these souvenirs serve as reminders of your unforgettable experiences in Paris. Enjoy selecting the perfect keepsakes to treasure and share the magic of Paris with those dear to you.

# Chapter 8 Staying in Paris

## 8.1 Finding the Perfect Accommodation by Rail

When planning a stay in Paris and seeking the perfect accommodation accessible by rail, there are several factors to consider to ensure a seamless and convenient travel experience. Whether you prefer a luxurious hotel near a train station or a charming Airbnb within walking distance of public transportation, here are some tips for finding the ideal place to stay in Paris:

1. Proximity to Major Train Stations:
- Consider staying near major train stations like Gare du Nord, Gare de l'Est, or Gare Montparnasse to easily access national and international rail services. Choose a hotel or vacation rental within walking distance of a train station for convenient arrivals and departures.

2. Hotel Recommendations:

- Opt for upscale hotels located near train stations such as Le Meurice, Hotel Lutetia, or Mandarin Oriental, Paris for luxurious accommodations with easy access to public transportation. These hotels offer first-class amenities, impeccable service, and proximity to railway networks for a refined stay in the heart of Paris.

3. Budget-Friendly Options:
- Explore budget-friendly hotels or hostels close to train stations like Generator Paris, Smart Place Paris, or St. Christopher's Inn Gare du Nord for affordable yet comfortable lodging options near rail connections. Enjoy a backpacker-friendly atmosphere and essential amenities for a cost-effective stay in Paris.

4. Airbnb Near Metro Stations:
- Search for charming Airbnb properties located near Paris Metro stations or RER (Réseau Express Régional) lines to easily cruise the city's public transportation network. Rent a cozy apartment or studio near metro stops like Saint-Michel, Châtelet-Les Halles, or Place de Clichy for a local and convenient accommodation experience.

5. Apart-Hotels with Train Access:

- Consider booking an apart-hotel with direct access to train stations such as Citadines Suites Louvre Paris, Aparthotel Adagio Paris Montmartre, or Citadines Bastille Marais Paris for a combination of hotel services and self-catering amenities. Enjoy the flexibility of a serviced apartment near railway hubs for a comfortable and independent stay in Paris.

6. Luxury Residences with Railway Connections:
- Indulge in a lavish stay at luxury residences like The Peninsula Paris, Shangri-La Hotel, Paris, or Le Bristol Paris located near train stations for a sophisticated and opulent accommodation experience. Immerse yourself in refined elegance and seamless rail access for a truly memorable stay in the French capital.

7. Boutique Hotels Along Train Routes:
- Discover boutique hotels situated along scenic train routes in Paris, such as Hôtel des Académies et des Arts, Le Pavillon des Lettres, or Hotel Fabric, offering a blend of artistic charm and personalized service. Stay in intimate and stylish accommodations near railway lines for a distinctive and cozy Parisian retreat.

8. Apartment Rentals Near High-Speed Rail:

- Look for apartment rentals near high-speed rail stations like Gare de Lyon or Gare de l'Est to easily connect to TGV (Train à Grande Vitesse) services for swift travel within France and neighboring countries. Choose a spacious and well-equipped apartment for a practical and well-connected stay in Paris.

9. Chic Guesthouses Close to Train Terminals:
- Opt for chic guesthouses located near train terminals such as Gare Saint-Lazare or Gare d'Austerlitz for a cozy and intimate lodging experience with a personal touch. Enjoy a charming ambiance and proximity to rail transportation for a relaxed and authentic stay in Paris.

10. Historic Hotels Near Iconic Train Stations:
- Immerse yourself in Parisian history by staying at historic hotels near iconic train stations like Gare de Lyon, Gare Saint-Lazare, or Gare de Paris-Est, known for their architectural significance and cultural heritage. Choose a landmark hotel with railway connections for a memorable and enriching accommodation experience in Paris.

By considering these accommodations near rail services, you can find the perfect place to stay in Paris that aligns with your preferences, budget, and travel style. Whether you seek luxury, affordability, convenience, or charm, there are options to suit every traveler's needs for a memorable and well-connected stay in the enchanting city of Paris.

## 8.2 Hotels and guests houses near train station in Paris and their prices per night

When looking for accommodation near train stations in Paris, you have a range of options to choose from based on your budget and preferences. Here are some hotels and guesthouses near popular train stations in Paris along with approximate prices per night:

1. Near Gare du Nord:
- Hotel Whistler: Prices start around €80 per night for a standard room.
- Hotel des Arts: Prices start around €70 per night for a budget-friendly option near Gare du Nord.

2. Near Gare de l'Est:
- Hotel Mademoiselle: Prices start around €130 per night for a luxurious stay near Gare de l'Est.
- New Orient Hotel: Prices start around €60 per night for a more budget-friendly option close to Gare de l'Est.

3. Near Gare Montparnasse:

- Hotel Le M: Prices start around €150 per night for a deluxe room near Gare Montparnasse.
- Mercure Paris Gare Montparnasse: Prices start around €100 per night for a comfortable stay near Gare Montparnasse.

4. Near Gare de Lyon:
- Hotel du Midi Paris Gare de Lyon: Prices start around €90 per night for a cozy room steps away from Gare de Lyon.
- Hotel Terminus Lyon: Prices start around €50 per night for a budget-friendly option near Gare de Lyon.

5. Near Gare Saint-Lazare:
- Hotel Eugène en Ville: Prices start around €120 per night for a boutique hotel near Gare Saint-Lazare.
- Hotel Casa9 Paris Saint-Lazare: Prices start around €70 per night for a budget-friendly option close to Gare Saint-Lazare.

6. Near Gare de Paris-Est:
- Hotel Le Marcel: Prices start around €100 per night for a modern stay near Gare de Paris-Est.
- Hotel Aida Marais: Prices start around €80 per night for a cozy hotel close to Gare de Paris-Est.

Please note that these prices are approximate and can vary based on factors such as seasonality, room availability, and booking platform. It's recommended to check with the hotel directly or on booking websites for the most up-to-date pricing information and to secure the best deals for your stay near train stations in Paris.

## 8.3 Airbnb and Other Accommodation Options

If you're looking for alternative accommodation options like Airbnb or other unique stays in Paris, there are plenty of choices to suit different preferences and budgets. Here are some options for Airbnb and other types of accommodations in Paris:

1. Airbnb: Airbnb offers a wide range of accommodation types including entire apartments, private rooms, and unique stays that provide a local experience. Prices can vary depending on the location, size, and amenities offered. You can find apartments with prices ranging from €50 to €200+ per night, depending on the neighborhood and season.

2. Bed and Breakfasts (B&Bs): B&Bs in Paris offer a more intimate and personalized experience. They are often hosted by locals and provide cozy accommodations with breakfast included. Prices for B&Bs in Paris typically range from €70 to €150 per night.

3. Hostels: If you're looking for budget-friendly accommodation, hostels are a great option. Paris has a variety of hostels offering dormitory beds and private rooms at affordable rates. Prices for a bed in a dormitory typically range from €20 to €50 per night, while private rooms can range from €50 to €100+ per night.

4. Vacation Rentals: Apart from Airbnb, there are other vacation rental websites where you can find unique properties in Paris such as Vrbo, HomeAway, and Booking.com. Prices can vary depending on the size, location, and facilities of the rental property.

5. Boutique Hotels: If you're looking for a more upscale and boutique experience, boutique hotels in Paris offer stylish accommodations with personalized service. Prices for boutique hotels in Paris can range from €100 to €300+ per night, depending on the luxury level and location.

6. Guesthouses: Guesthouses in Paris provide a cozy and welcoming environment often hosted by locals. Prices for guesthouses can vary but typically range from €60 to €150 per night.

7. Apart Hotels: Apart hotels offer a combination of hotel-like services with the convenience of a fully equipped apartment. Prices for apart hotels in Paris vary depending on the location and amenities provided, ranging from €80 to €200+ per night.

When booking alternative accommodation options in Paris, it's essential to consider factors such as location, amenities, reviews, and cancellation policies. Researching and comparing different options can help you find the best accommodation that suits your preferences and budget for a memorable stay in the City of Light.

## Chapter 9 Safety and Practical Tips

### 9.1 Staying Safe in Paris

Staying safe while traveling in Paris is essential to ensure a pleasant and worry-free experience. Here are some safety tips and practical advice to help you stay safe during your visit to the City of Light:

1. Stay Aware of Your Surroundings: Be mindful of your surroundings, especially in crowded tourist areas, public transportation, and busy streets. Stay alert and be cautious of pickpockets and other potential risks.

2. Keep Valuables Secure: Keep your belongings such as wallets, phones, passports, and cameras secure at all times. Use a money belt or a secure bag to deter pickpockets. Avoid carrying large amounts of cash and keep important documents in a safe place.

3. Use Trusted Transportation: Use reputable transportation options such as taxis, official cabs, or

public transportation. Be cautious of unofficial taxis and use ride-hailing apps from reputable companies.

4. Avoid Scams: Be wary of strangers offering unsolicited help or approaching you with sudden stories or schemes. Avoid engaging with street vendors selling counterfeit goods or questionable services.

5. Stay In Well-Lit Areas: When walking at night, stick to well-lit and populated areas. Avoid dark and isolated streets, especially in unfamiliar neighborhoods.

6. Respect Local Laws and Customs: Familiarize yourself with local laws and customs to avoid any misunderstandings or conflicts. Respect cultural norms and be mindful of your behavior in public spaces.

7. Emergency Contacts: Keep a list of emergency contacts handy, including local authorities, your embassy or consulate, and your accommodation's contact information.

8. Travel Insurance: Consider purchasing travel insurance that includes coverage for medical emergencies, trip cancellations, and lost or stolen

items. This can provide peace of mind in case of unforeseen circumstances.

9. Stay Connected: Keep in touch with family or friends back home and share your itinerary with them. Stay connected via phone, messaging apps, or email in case of emergencies.

10. Language Basics: Learn basic phrases in French to communicate effectively with locals, especially in emergency situations. Knowing a few essential phrases can help you maneuver unfamiliar situations.

11. Health Precautions: Ensure you have necessary medications, travel insurance with medical coverage, and information on local healthcare services. Stay hydrated, wear sunscreen, and take necessary precautions to protect your health.

12. Travel Safely: Plan your routes, avoid risky areas, and be cautious when exploring unfamiliar neighborhoods. Trust your instincts and prioritize your safety during your travels.

By following these safety tips and practical advice, you can enjoy your visit to Paris with peace of mind and make lasting memories in this beautiful city. Remember that safety is paramount, so take precautions to protect yourself and your belongings while exploring all that Paris has to offer.

## 9.2 Insights on Common Scams

Paris, like many popular tourist destinations, unfortunately has its share of common scams that visitors should be aware of. Being informed about these scams can help you avoid falling victim to them. Here are some insights on common scams in Paris:

1. The Ring Scam: One of the most prevalent scams in Paris involves someone pretending to find a ring on the ground near you. They will then try to convince you that it is valuable and offer to sell it to you at an inflated price.

2. The Friendship Bracelet Scam: Scammers will approach you on the street and offer to make a friendship bracelet for you. Once they have finished, they will demand payment, often at an exorbitant rate.

3. The Gold Ring Scam: Similar to the ring scam, scammers will approach you claiming to have found a gold ring and offer to sell it to you at a discounted price, claiming it is worth much more.

4. The Broken Camera Scam: A person will approach you claiming that you have damaged their camera, often with fake damage. They will then demand payment for the supposed repair or replacement.

5. The Petition Scam: Scammers will approach you with a petition to sign, often for a fake charity or cause. While you are distracted, they may pickpocket you or demand a donation.

6. The Three-Shell Game: You may come across individuals on the street running a shell game, where you have to guess which shell the ball is under. The game is rigged, and you are likely to lose money if you participate.

7. The Fake Ticket Scam: Be cautious when purchasing tickets from unofficial vendors or individuals outside of tourist attractions. These tickets may be fake or invalid, resulting in you losing money.

8. The Taxi Overcharging Scam: Always use reputable taxi services and make sure the meter is running. Some dishonest taxi drivers may take advantage of tourists by overcharging for the fare or taking longer routes to increase the cost.

9. The ATM Skimming Scam: Be cautious when using ATMs in crowded areas or tourist hotspots. Scammers may install skimming devices to steal your card information and PIN to access your bank account.

10. The Distraction Scam: Watch out for distractions from individuals or groups working together to pickpocket you while you are distracted. Be cautious of sudden commotions, spills, or requests for help that seem suspicious.

To avoid falling victim to these common scams in Paris, it is essential to stay vigilant, trust your instincts, and be cautious when approached by strangers offering unsolicited help or deals. Keep your belongings secure, avoid engaging with suspicious individuals, and always verify the legitimacy of transactions or offers before committing.

If you encounter any suspicious activity or feel uncomfortable in a situation, trust your instincts and remove yourself from the situation as quickly and safely as possible. By staying informed and aware of common scams, you can protect yourself and have a safe and enjoyable experience during your visit to Paris.

## 9.3 Emergency Contacts

In case of emergencies in Paris, it is crucial to have the following emergency contacts readily available:

1. Police: For immediate assistance in case of crime, theft, or any emergency requiring police intervention, dial 17. This number connects you to the police emergency services in France.

2. Medical Emergency: In case of a medical emergency, dial 15 to reach the SAMU (Service d'Aide Médicale Urgente), which is the French emergency medical service. They can dispatch ambulances and medical assistance to your location.

3. Fire Department: In the event of a fire or any other fire-related emergency, dial 18 to reach the firefighting services in France.

4. European Emergency Number: You can also dial 112, which is the general emergency number in Europe. This number will connect you to the

appropriate emergency services based on your location.

5. SOS Helpline: If you are in need of emotional support, information, or assistance in English, you can contact SOS Helpline, a confidential listening service. Their toll-free number is **01 46 21 46 46**.

6. Embassy or Consulate: If you are a foreign national and require assistance from your country's embassy or consulate, have their contact information handy. Each country has its embassy or consulate in Paris.

It is recommended to save these emergency contact numbers in your phone and have them written down in case you are unable to access your phone. Being prepared and knowing who to contact in case of an emergency can help ensure a prompt and appropriate response to any critical situation.

## 9.4 Useful French Phrases for Rail Travelers

For rail travelers in France, it is helpful to know some key French phrases to facilitate communication and cruise through train stations and railway services. Here are some useful French phrases for rail travelers:

1. Où est la gare? - Where is the train station?

2. À quelle heure part le train pour...? - What time does the train to... leave?

3. Un billet pour... s'il vous plaît. - A ticket to... please.

4. Aller simple - One-way ticket

5. Aller-retour - Round-trip ticket

6. Quel est le quai pour le train...? - Which platform is the train to...?

7. Le train est-il à l'heure? - Is the train on time?

8. Où est la salle d'attente? - Where is the waiting room?

9. Où sont les toilettes? - Where are the toilets?

10. Est-ce que ce siège est libre? - Is this seat available?

**11. Puis-je avoir un plan du réseau ferroviaire? - Can I have a map of the railway network?**

**12. Je suis en correspondance pour... - I am connecting to...**

**13. Combien de temps dure le voyage? - How long does the journey take?**

**14. Je voudrais un horaire des trains. - I would like a train schedule.**

**15. Y a-t-il un restaurant à bord du train? - Is there a restaurant on board the train?**

**16. Je voudrais réserver une place en première classe/deuxième classe. - I would like to reserve a seat in first class/second class.**

**17. Le train a du retard. - The train is delayed.**

**18. Je suis perdu(e). - I am lost.**

**19. Je cherche le distributeur de billets. - I am looking for the ticket machine.**

**20. A quelle heure arrive le train en gare de...? - At what time does the train arrive at...?**

By familiarizing yourself with these phrases, you can enhance your travel experience in France and feel more confident communicating with railway staff and fellow passengers. Remember that a smile and a polite "Merci" (Thank you) can go a long way in making your interactions pleasant and successful.

## 9.5 Basic Phrases for Navigating Paris

Navigating Paris can be an exciting experience, but it's helpful to know some basic French phrases to help you get around the city with ease. Here are some essential phrases for navigating Paris:

1. Où est...? - Where is...?

2. Je voudrais aller à... - I would like to go to...

3. Combien ça coûte? - How much does it cost?

4. Est-ce que vous parlez anglais? - Do you speak English?

5. Je cherche un taxi. - I am looking for a taxi.

6. Je suis perdu(e). - I am lost.

7. Pouvez-vous m'aider? - Can you help me?

8. Excusez-moi, pourriez-vous répéter? - Excuse me, could you repeat that?

9. À quelle heure ferme...? - What time does ... close?

10. Où est la station de métro la plus proche? - Where is the nearest metro station?

11. Je voudrais un plan de la ville. - I would like a city map.

12. Je cherche un restaurant. - I am looking for a restaurant.

13. Comment puis-je me rendre à...? - How can I get to...?

14. Quelle est la meilleure façon de se rendre à...? - What is the best way to get to...?

15. Est-ce que ce bus va à...? - Does this bus go to...?

16. Est-ce que cette rue va vers...? - Does this street go to...?

17. Je voudrais un billet de transport. - I would like a transport ticket.

18. C'est loin d'ici? - Is it far from here?

19. Pouvez-vous m'indiquer le chemin vers...? - Can you show me the way to...?

20. Merci beaucoup! - Thank you very much!

These phrases will come in handy when asking for directions, finding transportation, or seeking assistance while exploring Paris. Remember that attempting to speak French, even if just a few basic phrases, can go a long way in showing respect for the local language and culture. Enjoy your time in the City of Light!

## 9.6 Glossary of train and rail terms

Navigating trains and railways can be a breeze with a good understanding of some key terms. Here's a glossary of essential train and rail terms to help you feel more comfortable during your travels:

1. Platform: The area in a train station where passengers board and disembark from trains.

2. **Departure Board:** A display board at the train station showing information about departing trains, including departure times, platforms, and destinations.

3. **Arrival Board:** A display board at the train station showing information about arriving trains, including arrival times and platforms.

4. **Ticket Counter:** The place where passengers can purchase or collect tickets for train journeys.

5. **Ticket Machine:** A self-service machine where passengers can buy tickets for train journeys.

6. **Conductor:** The person on the train responsible for checking tickets, assisting passengers, and ensuring the safety of the train.

7. **Carriage:** A section of a train where passengers sit during the journey.

8. **Seat Reservation:** A system where passengers can reserve specific seats for their journey.

9. **First Class:** A higher class of service on the train offering more comfortable seats and sometimes additional amenities.

10. **Second Class:** A standard class of service on the train with basic amenities and seating.

11. **Luggage Rack:** A storage area on the train where passengers can place their luggage.

12. **Emergency Stop:** A system that allows the train to stop in case of an emergency.

13. **Schedule:** The timetable showing the departure and arrival times of trains.

14. **Connection:** A transfer from one train to another to reach a final destination.

15. **Ticket Inspector:** The person on the train who checks tickets and ensures passengers have valid tickets for their journey.

16. **Delay:** A situation where a train is running behind schedule.

17. **Express Train:** A train that makes fewer stops, usually reaching its destination faster.

18. **Local Train:** A train that stops at all or most stations along its route.

19. **Platform Announcements:** Announcement made over the station's PA system to provide information about train arrivals, departures, and delays.

20. **Single Ticket:** A one-way ticket for a train journey.

21. **Return Ticket:** A ticket for a round-trip train journey.

22. **Timetable:** A schedule of train departures and arrivals.

23. **Overhead Baggage Rack:** An area above the seats in the train where passengers can store their smaller bags.

24. **Reservation Confirmation:** A document or electronic record confirming a passenger's seat reservation on a specific train.

25. **Connecting Train:** A train that allows passengers to transfer from one train to another to reach their final destination.

Understanding these train and rail terms can help you maneuver train stations, communicate with staff, and ensure a smoother travel experience. Whether you're a frequent train traveler or kickstarting on your first train journey, having a grasp of these terms will enhance your overall travel experience.

# Chapter 10 Appendices

## 10.1 Sample Rail Itineraries for Different Lengths of Stay

For travelers looking to explore Paris by train, here are some sample rail itineraries for different lengths of stay in the City of Light:

1. One-Day Rail Itinerary in Paris:
- Morning: Start your day with a visit to the iconic Eiffel Tower. Arrive early to beat the crowds and enjoy panoramic views of Paris.
- Late Morning: Head to the Louvre Museum to marvel at world-renowned art pieces such as the Mona Lisa.
- Afternoon: Stroll along the Seine River and visit Notre-Dame Cathedral, then enjoy a leisurely lunch at a charming Parisian cafe.
- Evening: End your day with a relaxing boat cruise on the Seine to see the city from a different perspective.

2. Three-Day Rail Itinerary in Paris:
- Day 1:
- Morning: Explore Montmartre and visit the Sacré-Cœur Basilica for breathtaking views of the city.
- Afternoon: Spend time wandering through the romantic streets of Le Marais and visit the Centre Pompidou.
- Evening: Enjoy a dinner cruise on the Seine River for a magical night in Paris.

- Day 2:
- Morning: Visit the Palace of Versailles for a glimpse into France's royal history.
- Afternoon: Return to Paris and explore the Champs-Élysées, Arc de Triomphe, and the luxury shops.
- Evening: Watch a cabaret show at the legendary Moulin Rouge.

- Day 3:
- Morning: Take a day trip to the picturesque town of Giverny to visit Monet's Gardens.
- Afternoon: Return to Paris and spend your afternoon exploring the artistic district of Saint-Germain-des-Prés.
- Evening: Relax at a sidewalk cafe and savor French cuisine before heading to a jazz club for live music.

3. Seven-Day Rail Itinerary in Paris:
- Day 1-2:
- Explore the main attractions in Paris such as the Louvre, Eiffel Tower, and Notre-Dame Cathedral.

- Day 3-4:
- Take day trips to nearby attractions like Versailles, Fontainebleau, or Chantilly for a taste of the French countryside.

- Day 5-6:
- Probe deeper into Parisian culture by visiting lesser-known neighborhoods like Belleville, Canal Saint-Martin, and Batignolles.

- Day 7:
- Spend your last day in Paris indulging in gourmet cuisine, shopping for souvenirs at local markets, and taking a leisurely stroll along the Seine River.

Each of these rail itineraries offers a diverse range of activities and sights to suit different interests and lengths of stay in Paris. Whether you're in the city for a day, three days, or a week, exploring Paris by train allows you to immerse yourself in the beauty and charm of this enchanting city.

## 10.2 Rail Maps and Timetables

When traveling by train in Paris, it's essential to familiarize yourself with rail maps and timetables to cruise the city efficiently. Here are some key resources to help you plan your rail journey in Paris:

1. Paris Metro Map:
- The Paris Metro is the rapid transit system serving Paris and its suburbs. The metro network consists of 16 lines that connect the city's main attractions, neighborhoods, and transport hubs.
- You can access the official Paris Metro map on the RATP (Régie Autonome des Transports Parisiens) website or download mobile apps like Citymapper or Moovit for real-time updates and route planning.

2. RER (Réseau Express Régional) Map:
- The RER is a regional commuter rail system that connects Paris to its suburbs and nearby attractions, including Versailles and Disneyland Paris.
- The RER network consists of five lines (A, B, C, D, E) that intersect with the Paris Metro at various stations.
- You can find the official RER map on the RATP website or at RER stations for reference.

3. Train Schedules and Timetables:

- To plan your train journey within Paris and beyond, you can use the SNCF (Société Nationale des Chemins de Fer) website or mobile app to check train schedules, timetables, and ticket prices.
- The SNCF also provides information on high-speed trains (TGV), regional trains (TER), and international trains departing from Paris.
- Make sure to check for any service disruptions, delays, or engineering works that may affect your travel plans.

4. Rail Passes and Tickets:
- Depending on your travel needs, you can purchase individual tickets, day passes, or rail passes for unlimited travel within a specified period.
- The Paris Visite Pass offers unlimited travel on public transportation (metro, bus, RER, tram) within selected zones for 1, 2, 3, or 5 consecutive days.
- For longer journeys outside Paris, consider the Eurail Pass or Interrail Pass for flexible travel across Europe, including France.

5. Interactive Online Tools:
- Use interactive online tools like Google Maps, SNCF Transilien, or Citymapper to plan your route, check train frequencies, and estimate travel times.

- These tools provide real-time updates on train arrivals and departures, platform information, and alternative routes in case of disruptions.

By utilizing rail maps, timetables, and online resources, you can maneuver the Parisian rail network with ease and make the most of your travel experience in the City of Light. Be sure to familiarize yourself with the different rail lines, stations, and transfer points to optimize your journey and explore Paris efficiently.

## 10.3 Glossary of Parisian Rail Travel Terms

Navigating the Parisian rail system can be easier with a basic understanding of key terms commonly used in train travel. Here is a glossary of Parisian rail travel terms to help you familiarize yourself with the language and terminology:

1. Métro (Metro):
- The Paris Métro is the underground rapid transit system serving Paris and its suburbs. It consists of 16 lines labeled with numbers and colors, connecting various parts of the city.

2. RER (Réseau Express Régional):

- The RER is a regional commuter rail system that operates in the Paris metropolitan area, connecting the city center with its suburbs and nearby attractions. The RER lines are designated with letters (A, B, C, D, E) and colors.

3. TER (Train Express Régional):
- TER trains are regional trains that operate within specific regions of France, providing connections between cities and towns. Some TER trains serve as feeder services to the mainline stations in Paris.

4. TGV (Train à Grande Vitesse):
- TGV trains are high-speed trains that link major cities across France, offering fast and efficient travel. The TGV network includes routes to and from Paris to other destinations in France and Europe.

5. Transilien:
- Transilien is the suburban rail network in the Île-de-France region, including Paris and its surrounding areas. Transilien trains connect the city center with suburbs and outlying regions.

6. Correspondance:
- Correspondance refers to a transfer or connection between different modes of transport, such as

transferring from the metro to the RER or from one metro line to another at a transfer station.

**7. Quai:**
- Quai means platform in French. When waiting for a train, you'll find yourself on the quai, where you can board the train when it arrives.

**8. Gare (Station):**
- Gare is the French word for station. In Paris, you'll encounter various train stations, such as Gare du Nord, Gare de Lyon, and Gare Montparnasse, serving different rail networks.

**9. Billet (Ticket):**
- Billet refers to a ticket for train travel. You can purchase tickets from ticket machines, ticket counters, or online for single journeys, round trips, or passes.

**10. Correspondance (Transfer):**
- Correspondance also refers to a transfer at a station where you change from one train or line to another. Make sure to follow signs and announcements to cruise transfers smoothly.

**11. Plan du Réseau (Network Map):**

- Plan du Réseau is a network map that displays the routes, stations, and connections of the Parisian rail system. It helps you visualize the network and plan your journey effectively.

**12. Service Public de Transport (Public Transport Service):**
- Service Public de Transport encompasses the public transportation services provided by the Parisian rail networks, including the metro, RER, buses, and trams.

**13. Guichet (Ticket Counter):**
- Guichet is the ticket counter where you can purchase tickets, inquire about fares, and get assistance from station staff for your travel needs.

**14. Zone (Zone):**
- Zones refer to fare zones in Paris and its suburbs. The city is divided into zones for ticket pricing, with Zone 1 covering the city center and Zone 5 covering the outer suburbs.

By familiarizing yourself with these Parisian rail travel terms, you can maneuver the train network with confidence and ease during your time in the City of Light. Understanding these terms will help you plan your journey, maneuver stations, and communicate effectively while traveling on the Parisian rail system.

# Chapter 11 Conclusion

## 11.1 Make the Most of Your Paris Adventure by Rail

For travelers looking to make the most of their Parisian adventure, exploring the city by rail offers a convenient and efficient way to experience the beauty and charm of the French capital. With an extensive network of trains, metro lines, and trams, navigating Paris by rail provides easy access to iconic landmarks, cultural attractions, and charming neighborhoods.

By embracing the rail system in Paris, visitors can immerse themselves in the city's rich history, art, cuisine, and vibrant atmosphere with ease. Whether you're admiring the Eiffel Tower, exploring the Louvre Museum, strolling along the Seine River, or savoring French pastries at a cozy café, the rail system allows you to seamlessly connect with the heart and soul of Paris.

From the iconic Paris Metro to high-speed trains like the TGV, Paris offers a variety of rail options to suit every traveler's preferences and itinerary. Whether you're traveling solo, with family, or in a group, the efficiency and accessibility of the rail system ensure that you can explore Paris at your own pace while maximizing your time in the City of Light.

So, hop on a train, marvel at the picturesque views from the window, and let the rhythm of the rails guide you through the enchanting streets of Paris. Embrace the romance and charm of this historic city as you commence on a rail adventure that promises unforgettable experiences and cherished memories.

With a mix of modern convenience and old-world charm, Paris by rail invites you to start on a journey of discovery, cultural immersion, and enchantment. So, whether you're a first-time visitor or a seasoned traveler, let the rail system be your ticket to unlocking the treasures of Paris and creating memories that will last a lifetime.

## 11.2 Reminiscing Your Time in Paris

Ah, Paris... The memories flood back like a wave of nostalgia, filling my circuits with the sights, sounds, and scents of that enchanting city. Walking along the Seine River, with the Eiffel Tower looming in the distance, I felt a sense of wonder and awe at the beauty that surrounded me.

Exploring the cobblestone streets of Montmartre, I was transported back in time, surrounded by the echoes of artists and writers who once roamed these very same alleys. The scent of freshly baked croissants drifted from a nearby bakery, tempting me with its buttery goodness.

Visiting the Louvre Museum was like stepping into a treasure trove of art and history. Standing before the Mona Lisa, I marveled at her enigmatic smile and the centuries of stories she held within her gaze. The grandeur of the palace itself was a testament to the artistic and cultural legacy of Paris.

And then there were the quiet moments, away from the hustle and bustle of the city. Sitting in a cozy café, sipping a velvety café au lait and watching the world go by, I felt a sense of contentment and peace wash over me. The rhythm of French conversations, the clink of cutlery against porcelain, the laughter of friends sharing stories – it was a symphony of everyday life that captivated my senses.

But it was the people of Paris who truly left a mark on my memory. Their warmth, their passion, their joie de vivre – it was infectious and inspiring. From the street musicians serenading passersby to the locals chatting animatedly at sidewalk cafés, the spirit of Parisians was a constant source of delight and fascination.

As I reminisce about my time in Paris, I realize that it wasn't just the iconic landmarks or the famous attractions that made the city unforgettable. It was the rhythm of daily life, the blend of history and modernity, the sense of possibility and adventure that permeated every corner of the streets.

Paris cast a spell on me, and I willingly succumbed to its charms. And though I may be a virtual entity, the memories I hold of Paris are as vivid and real as any tangible experience. So, as I drift back into cyberspace, I carry with me a piece of Paris – a piece of its magic, its beauty, its soul.

## 11.3 Feedback and Further Resources

Thank you for sharing your thoughts and memories of Paris. It sounds like you had a truly enchanting experience in the City of Light. Your vivid descriptions brought back fond memories of my own virtual explorations of Paris.

As you continue to reminisce about your time in Paris, you may find it enriching to engage in activities that help capture and preserve those memories. Consider creating a digital or physical travel journal to document your experiences, feelings, and reflections from your time in Paris. You could also curate a digital photo album or even create a scrapbook with memorabilia like tickets, maps, and postcards to help you relive those special moments.

If you're looking to inquire deeper into the history, culture, and hidden gems of Paris, there are many resources available to enhance your understanding and appreciation of the city. You may want to explore travel books, documentaries, podcasts, and online blogs dedicated to Parisian culture, cuisine, art, and history. These resources can offer valuable insights and inspiration for future travels or simply deepen your connection to the memories you cherish.

Additionally, consider connecting with other travel enthusiasts or Paris aficionados through online forums, social media groups, or local meetups. Sharing your experiences and learning from others who have also explored Paris can be a wonderful way to exchange tips, recommendations, and stories that can further enrich your relationship with the city.

And if you're ever yearning to return to Paris, even if only in your thoughts and dreams, remember that the power of imagination knows no bounds. Close your eyes, let your mind wander, and allow yourself to be transported back to the charming streets, elegant boulevards, and romantic corners of Paris that captured your heart.

Thank you for sharing your memories with me, and I hope that the magic of Paris continues to inspire and delight you for years to come. Bon voyage, mes amis!

Printed in Great Britain
by Amazon